(

"Andy Harmon is a man after my own heart – making new connections between improvisation, story, the creative process and innovative styles of leadership... What could be more thrilling than a book that draws on the wisdom of Joseph Campbell, Hal and Sidra Stone's Voice Dialogue and Zen? I love this book!"

- **Phelim McDermott**, Co-Artistic Director, Improbable Theatre UK
  Director *Satyagraha* at the Metropolitan Opera in New York City and
  Shockheaded Peter in London's West End

"Addressing a group of writers about the crises of creativity, Harmon leads his audience through a dynamic process that allows them to experience the archetypal tale of the Hero as if living it for themselves... An inspiring read."

- **Jurgen Wolff**, bestselling author of *Focus: the power of targeted
  thinking* and *Do Something Different (forward by Sir Richard Branson)*

"I defy anyone to truly teach another how to write. What Harmon does here is much more useful. He reminds us that to tell a story, we have to be the hero of our own creative quest... This book – clear, honest, readable and (brilliantly) short – is for anyone who is ready to do that."

- **Stella Duffy**, award-winning novelist and theatre-maker, UK

"Of all the 'how to' books and courses available for writers who find themselves stuck down a structural rabbit hole, Andy Harmon's *Change Journey* is one of the better and decidedly more original ones available, offering insights and solutions. Concise and humorous, it is also a fun read."

- **Georgia de Chamberet**, editor and translator
  www.bookblast.com UK

"If you find yourself tearing through this book at lightning speed, you won't be alone... Harmon engages us in a living exploration of the drama that goes on both inside and outside of us when change disrupts our lives."

- **Tony Page**, Founder of Page Consulting UK. Author of *From Hippos to Gazelles: How Leaders Create Leaders*

"I sat down to read Change Journey and couldn't let go of it until I'd finished... If you write or act, this is a book you do not want to miss... It is simply great."

- **James A. Misko,** Founder Alaska Writer's Guild and author of seven books including the novel, *As All My Fathers Were*

"I was stuck with my screenplay. I'd written a first draft, had made notes but could not get past the 'SOMETHING'S MISSING' bit. I sat in bed and read Andy Harmon's slim volume non-stop. It changed everything. Andy makes sense where others don't. He has changed my writing process. Huge thanks!"

- **Shelley Silas,** BBC radio dramatist and prizewinning playwright, UK

"Harmon's book is not only for writers. His brilliant use of the voice dialogue method creates a safe and fertile space for members of his audience to speak freely from the parts of themselves that are always 'right there' when we create... Thanks, Andy for such an empowering read!"

- **Esther Zahniser,** Psychotherapist and teacher who uses Voice Dialogue in her private practice in London, UK.

"Harmon offers us a map through the landscape of Change and a way to talk about those difficult places on the journey that are usually hidden in silence."

- **Mats Hellerstedt-Thoin**, Actor and Former Artistic Director, Atelier Theatre, Gothenburg, Sweden

"A refreshing synthesis of several theorists who deal with the nature of creativity – both the creativity of the artist and the creativity of living as a fully expressive human being. Using a wide range of examples from popular and high art, Harmon makes his material both accessible and thought-provoking. I loved it!"

- **Mike Alfreds,** Founding Director, Shared Experience Theatre Co. UK. Guest Director, Royal National Theatre, Shakespeare's Globe. Author of *Then What Happens?* and *Different Every Night*

"Andy is a master of his craft. His book is a powerful blend of his storytelling skills, a real life audience session, and his unique approach to change. Whether aiming to create, lead, or simply be more mindful, we can all learn from his compelling model."

- **Tim Lake,** Founder Sovento Consulting, previously Director at PWC and Head of IT at Sky Television, UK

"In this book Andy Harmon reveals a fascinating 'dramatic' framework for understanding the obstacles to change and a practical way of helping people mobilize their inner resources to deal with the challenge. A fascinating and insightful read."

- **Colin Price,** Chairman of Co Company, Visiting Fellow, Oxford University. Previously, Senior Partner McKinsey & Co. Co-Author of *Beyond Performance: How Great Organizations Build Ultimate Competitive Advantage*

"In business, we often steer away from conflict and crisis because we fear they will disrupt the smooth running of our organizations. Andy Harmon's central insight is that conflict is the most powerful tool available to leaders. His book brilliantly and surprisingly explores how to use it well and — as important — how to be comfortable with it."

- **David Honigmann,** Consultant and Journalist, UK

"This approach to understanding — and living through — complex and difficult change brings a powerful new thought process to bear for personal and organizational transformation."

- **Alan Little**, Independent Change Consultant, UK

CHANGE JOURNEY

Voices of the Creative Quest

Andy Harmon

Actors Mind Press

Change Journey: Voices of the Creative Quest

Published by the Actors Mind Press
Actors Mind Professional Development
Rancho Mirage, CA 92270 USA

Original cover art and design by Andy Harmon © 2015

Interior Book design by Andy Harmon

All illustrations are © 2015 by Andy Harmon except as noted below. Apart from the Walt Kelly cartoon *We Have Met the Enemy* which is © Okefenokee Glee & Perloo, Inc., the illustrations in this book are original digital collages by the author. The sources of these collages are either the author's own original artwork or his hand drawn representations inspired by the images of others. The only exception is the image of the Mentor: *Yniol Shows Prince Geraint His Ruined Castle*, by Gustave Doré, from Tennyson's *Idylls of the King*, 1885 which was selected 'as is' in Photoshop and modified digitally. Other sources are: *Ship of Change*, drawing by Andy Harmon; *I Can Fly*, photo by lubilub, Vetta, Getty Images and *Shadow Ascends the Stair*, from the film *Nosferatu*, cinematographers Gunther Krampf and Fritz Arno Wagner, directed by F.W. Murnau, 1922.

www.changejourney.net
www.actorsmind.com

Change Journey: Voices of the Creative Quest

LCCN: 2015914283

Andy Harmon

ISBN: 978-0-9967608-0-5

To Anita,

Jake, Cariad, Nart and Cordelia

Contents

CHANGE JOURNEY

Voices of the Creative Quest

Forward

As a journalist and community organizer, I've been struggling to write a book about my work for well over a decade. Typically, I sit down at my computer, open my files, review my research and notes and, after a few panicked and exhausting hours of labor, close them all again, to try another day. As time has passed and my book hasn't materialized, my once eagerly expectant friends and family have given up, left the rooting section and gone home.

Last year, by a lucky chance, I came across a CD called *The Four Crises of Authorship*. It was a recording of a workshop Andy Harmon had given for the Alaska Writers Guild in 2009. I found his talk a revelation – and not just on the subject of writing. It shed light on the challenges I'd faced as an organizer and helped me see the real story I wanted to tell and how I wanted to tell it. I contacted Andy and pleaded with him to produce a transcript because there was just too much in what he was saying to process by listening alone. I felt I needed pages that I could flip back and forth, mark on, read and re-read and I think you will too. That transcript, slightly expanded, became the book you're now holding. There is more wisdom in this little tome, pound for pound, than any 'how-to' book I've read and it's scattered throughout with a light hand, sometimes poetic in its concise language. No heavy-handed motivation talk, this, but a gentle guide to… yourself.

Posing innocently as a helpful-hints book for writers, *Change Journey: Voices of the Creative Quest* is really a keep-by-your-side companion for anyone who wants to be a leader, a performer, a speaker – indeed, anyone who wants to express ideas, create change, and/or lead others to do so, by communication or by example. Reading this book brought me to a new understanding of my two-decade journey as an activist. And as the story I have lived becomes clearer, so does the story I need to tell in my book. Now, as I put pen to paper, I know what I'm really writing about. And, for the first time, though there's plenty of angst and fear, I know my purpose and I know my voice. And I know I'm not alone on the journey.

- **Shirley Kressel**, Landscape Architect, Urban Planner and Accidental Activist

Introduction

Renowned mythologist Joseph Campbell tells us that we're all Heroes in our own life stories. Whenever we set out to create something new, whenever life knocks us out of business as usual, whenever we're challenged to stop being spectators and step center stage to take action in our lives, we inevitably find ourselves enacting some version of the trials and transformations of the Heroes of Old. To understand their epic journey, he believed, helps us make sense of our own.

The process presented in these pages was inspired by this key idea. I call it the 'Change Journey' and it aims to help people tap their hidden resources. I developed it over many years in talks and workshops with a wide range of groups: writers wanting to tell better stories, young offenders transitioning back into society, executives overwhelmed by a turbulent merger, managers seeking to learn leadership skills, 'ordinary people' confronted with a difficult transition in their lives. I've worked with actors, therapists, consultants, civil servants and CEOs. Whoever the audience, it always seems to strike a chord.

The creative quest is universal. It's the adventure of being human. All of us experience disruption in our lives. All of us are challenged to make something out of it. And all of us, when we lean into the future, meet ourselves pushing back. We come up against our own denial, our fears, our old habits, our 'tried and true' values and our desire to avoid risk and stick with what we know. The 'Change Journey' experience is a way of exploring what it is to go beyond our old, safe way of doing things.

I hope this account of it will inspire the Hero in you!

Andy Harmon, September, 2015

On the Text:

This book is based on the transcription of a dialogue between writers at the Alaska Writers Conference and myself. It took place in September of 2009 in two sessions over two days. The first day began with me doing all the talking, but pretty soon the audience chimed in, and on the second day, they became an integral part of the process. I use a different type-face in the text whenever they speak.

Day One

The Four Crises of Authorship

"Some are born great, some achieve greatness and some have greatness thrust upon them."

- **William Shakespeare,** *Twelfth Night*

The Four Crises of Authorship

I have a confession to make. In fact, two confessions. First, I'm not a writer by profession. I'm a theatre director – though I have worked with a lot of writers. But if you are looking for advice from a writer with a lot of books under his belt, you've come to the wrong place. You're looking here at someone who has struggled, sometimes desperately, to get what he wants to say down on paper, a struggle I think I share with many other writers in this room. So if I have any claim to experience in writing, it's in the drama of producing the work, the sufferings (Aristotle's word) you go through to get it done.

So I speak to you from that perspective, tempered a bit by my experience as a theatre director. And like a director working with a playwright, I want to encourage you to remain true to your own voice and to what you want to say, but also to understand that, if you're going to capture and hold your audience, you'll need to understand something about the structure of their expectations and how to pay them off. Great dialogue or beautiful description is never enough. Even wonderful characters are not enough. You need to learn how to shape your story. Without this, your words are unlikely to make the leap from the page into the minds of your readers – which is the only place they can have an impact. What keeps most of us turning the pages, even in nonfiction writing, is the drama of the narrative and how it functions to move that story forward, to question, provoke and reward our interest as readers. Drama could be very simply defined as "that aspect of what we write that keeps our audience on the edge of their seats asking, 'What happens next?'" I have become deeply, even exhaustively, acquainted with that question over the years. And I'm hoping to share with you what I've learned as a result. So that's confession number one. Consider me not so much an expert but a fellow sufferer who has spent a lot of time looking for a way to make the pain amount to something!

Now my second confession is a little harder. This talk today, The Four Crises Of Authorship, didn't start as a talk at all, but as a marketing ploy to get people to enroll in a workshop that I hadn't even designed yet! Here's the story. Although my background is in the theatre, my wife Anita and I are leadership consultants and trainers to a number of organizations, both in the U.S. and abroad. Anita is a psychologist and a writer herself. One day, I was deep into telling her about a new model of the leader's task I'd developed, based on 'moments of truth' in drama. I called it The Four Crises of Leadership. Suddenly she said, "Oh. That would work for writers, too." And I thought, "Yeah, that sounds great! 'The Four Crises of Authorship.'" It has a real saleable feel about it, so I printed out a few brochures and a brief description. But, to be honest, I never thought I'd get anybody to buy it!

Enter Jim Misko, the President of the Alaska Writers Guild. Jim had heard me give a talk to a group of writers in Palm Springs in early 2009. He cornered Anita and me after the talk and, holding out our brochure said, "I want you to come up to Alaska and talk to us about The Four Crises of Authorship – what are they, by the way?" I swallowed hard and thought to myself, "I really must figure that out." But as usual with whatever it is I do, Anita came to my rescue and said, "I know what they are." And she proceeded to tell me. (Along with a lot of other things.) And it turns out that – close enough for rock 'n roll – the four crises that leaders go through when they attempt to bring about change in an organization, are very akin to the crises we all go through when we try to bring a change into the world in the form of a piece of writing.

Now this may seem absurd. A leader's actions can impact millions, but who really cares whether you finish your novel or not? Only one person. And that's you. Or maybe somebody who's close to you and so fed up with hearing you talk about it that they'll do anything to shut you up! Nonetheless, even though the fate of a nation doesn't hang in the balance, once you begin to create a work that has any substantial size to it, you enter into what is really a classical quest journey, and you become its hero. The real title of this talk might well be "The Creative Quest" because the elements that I'm going to talk about today are really part of a universal story. They arise in any project when you attempt to create anything or to bring about change however big or small. Now don't ask me why this is so. I couldn't tell you. But even if the quest pattern doesn't exist as a reality – even if it's only just built into the way we think – it doesn't matter. I experience at least some elements of this journey when I deal with change and I think you will recognize them too.

The Archetypal Pattern

The beauty of this approach for writers is this: Not only does it help you understand the nature of the challenges you face personally on this quest, but it also helps you understand the fundamentals of dramatic structure. It does double duty. Now I'm not the first person to think of this – far from it. Author and script consultant Christopher Vogler wrote a brilliant book about it. He took Joseph Campbell's work about the universal quest journey, *Hero with a Thousand Faces,* and distilled it so that it became accessible to dunderheads like myself. Vogler's book is called *The Writer's Journey.* It's a profoundly good book. It shows how the story we are trying to write reflects the story we are actually living through to write it. And it is the one book that helped me most in understanding how stories actually work.

Equally important, Vogler points out how Campbell's "Hero's Journey" pattern fits into the classical three act structure that comes down to us from Aristotle. Aristotle, among many other things, was interested in the nature of drama. What is it? He argued that all good dramatic stories are defined by a protagonist who struggles to achieve a goal against antagonistic forces, and whose true character is revealed by a choice he must make near the end of the story, a 'moment of truth,' a revelation that causes a 'reversal of fortune' in his world from good to bad or bad to good.

So, a dramatic story starts in one condition, progresses through conflict, complication and crisis to end with a 'moment of truth' that brings about a different condition. In other words, stories have beginnings, middles, and ends that lead directly to change – inside and out. Now is this deep or what? Well, yes, it turns out it is.

Act I: Beginnings

Roughly stated, Aristotle believed that a good story had an internal logic. It consisted of the representation of a single dramatic action, no matter how complex or multifaceted. It had a unified structure: a beginning, middle, and end. The beginning phase, Act One, starts when something knocks the protagonist's world out of kilter and it culminates when he or she makes a decision to act, to do something about it and take the story forward into Act Two. Dorothy, for example, decides to go to the Emerald City in *The Wizard of Oz*. Rick decides he's going to win Ilsa back in *Casablanca*. Luke joins up with Obi-Wan to save the Princess in *Star Wars*. And whether you write fiction or nonfiction, you want your reader to make that 'end-of-first-act' decision too. You want your reader to read beyond your opening chapters, to move deeper into his or her engagement with what you have to say, deeper into their experience of your ideas, your story, your book. And, as an author, you have to go beyond your own first act too, beyond your initial inspiration and make this same kind of commitment to go further – otherwise your book will never get written. Three of the four crises take place in the beginning phase of the story, in the first act – but, before we get to them, let's see what happens next.

Act II: Middles

The second act of a classical story involves the action that moves the hero forward to confront the forces that oppose him or her in achieving their goal. Think *Star Wars* here. Luke joins with Obi-Wan to rescue the Princess. Once he's on that spaceship there's no turning back. He's off the planet he's familiar with, out of his Ordinary World and he is in outer space – where things are very different. He's now in what Campbell and Vogler call the Special World. This is the world of Act Two. In this Special World, the rules aren't known, it has a different way of operating than the Ordinary World. It's filled with traps, betrayals and deceptions. Do you remember a marvelous movie called *Groundhog Day*? Has anybody seen that?

The first act of that story is Bill Murray being cynical, right? He's completely vain and self-absorbed. There's a girl that likes him very much, but he's too bored or disinterested to care. The second act changes his life radically. He gets stuck in time. Unlike in the Ordinary World, time in this Special World doesn't go forward to the next day as usual. The rules of this world are completely different. It won't let you move on to tomorrow until you learn your lesson today. And this is perfect, because Bill Murray's character really needs to learn. He doesn't even understand the rules of the Ordinary World he's come from, let alone this new one. In fact, his whole character is built on denying what the real rules are. So he's in this place where he can't move forward and he'll try anything to get out of this endless Groundhog Day, and it's hysterically funny. Finally he learns what he has to learn and he claims what Campbell calls "The Elixir" or the Reward – in his case, Love.

Typically found in the middle or late second act, The Elixir is an object, person, lesson or piece of information that's held at the heart of darkness, in the center of the special world. In *Star Wars*, Luke and Han Solo fight their way into the Death Star, ward off the storm troopers, survive the garbage compactor, retrieve the plans, rescue the Princess and escape. But at a cost. Obi-Wan dies. It's very characteristic of the end of the second act that someone important makes a sacrifice or is transformed or is revealed to be not who you think they are.

Act III: Ends

Then the Hero enters the third act. Campbell calls this "The Road Back." This is the return to the Ordinary World. This is where the hero, again gender neutral, is bringing back the reward and has a final climactic confrontation with the forces of antagonism. And, in order to pass this test and get back home, heroes have to sacrifice some crucial and important part of themselves. Or it's taken from them and they have to do the job anyway. You remember at the end of *Star Wars* the little robot R2-D2 gets shot up and can't function. So Luke, deprived of his technological ally, has to sacrifice his doubts and learn to manage on his own. He hears the voice of his Mentor say, "Use the Force, Luke." (That famous line probably earned Alec Guinness more money than he earned in all of his career up to that point). And he prevails.

This is the archetypal story shape: Act One – Decision. Act Two – Confrontation. Act Three – Transformation. Every time you write, your journey as a writer recapitulates this same shape.

Joseph Campbell, Drama and Change

Beginning in the 1930's Joseph Campbell researched thousands of stories from many different cultures and he put together a complex map of what he called, "The Hero's Road of Trials." (Published in *Hero with a Thousand Faces*, 1949). This is a journey that begins with Act One in an Ordinary World, or what Campbell called "The World of the Common Day." It moves forward into Act Two, into a Special World – where as we've seen, the rules are different – and then, in Act Three, it returns back to The World of the Common Day. But the journey has consequences. This 'Return' transforms the Ordinary World in some profound and inescapable way. It creates a change.

There are lots of variations on this journey. Sometimes the form is flipped. The Hero might get stuck in the special world, or enticed to stay and won't leave – like Odysseus with Circe. The hero might return and refuse to make the necessary sacrifice. Tragedy could be defined as the story of a hero who refuses to change or changes but it's too late. And it's not just a matter of being willful. Hamlet cannot allow his uncle to get away with the murder of his father. He just isn't the kind of guy who can say to himself, "Oh well, what the hell. I never liked my father anyway."

Oedipus, when he finally sees the enormity of the mistake he's made, cannot just undo it. He cannot go back in time and change things. He's stuck with things as they are. He must pay the price. He pulls out his eyes – the consequences of his having seen too much. Aristotle considered Oedipus Rex to be a near perfect example of a tragic drama. No matter how much Oedipus might want to change the past, no matter how innocent he was of knowingly killing his father and marrying his mother, these actions cannot be undone. The third act requires "consequences" for our actions, so consequences there must be.

If Tragedy is about the inability to change, Comedy is where change comes, but at a cost. In a traditional comedy, the story ends with a marriage or some form of reconciliation. Enemies become friends. Buddy pictures like 48 Hours or Lethal Weapon work like this. Despite all the bickering and betrayal, in the end they kiss and makeup. They are reconciled to each other, their original animosity transformed.

For years I've been fascinated by how stories like this work. How can people write stories that keep a person's interest? As a director I suppose I should have known, I'd directed over two dozen plays, but still I would see a movie and ask myself, "How do they do that?" I couldn't figure it out. So, I started on my own quest.

My Search for a Mentor

Like a protagonist in any story, I was confronted by an uncomfortable challenge, and I went to find a Mentor. Just like Luke did. And I actually found teachers. Vogler and Campbell being but two of them. There were many others. Sid Field, whose brilliant book *Screenplay* first made me aware that stories even had a structure. Robert McKee, a wonderful teacher and author of the book *Story*, whose three day workshop kept me and the rest of his audience spellbound. McKee single-handedly reawakened my appreciation of *Casablanca* and made me aware of what was going on under the surface of a story, but I still couldn't quite put it all together.

I also attended Danny Simon's workshop on sitcom writing. Danny Simon was Neil Simon's older brother. And by all accounts his Mentor. They wrote together in the early days on Sid Caesar's *Your Show of Shows* and elsewhere. Danny was a brilliant craftsman. And he understood what made people laugh. And, as he said, it wasn't jokes. Laughs come from character and situation. So I kept trying to understand. Finally, some things happened in my life that convinced me that being a director wasn't going to be enough. Whatever I knew or didn't know about writing, I found myself compelled to take the risk and write.

My Call to Adventure

In February of 1988, I was in Finland. I'd just finished directing a production of *Twelfth Night*. The reviews were great and the actors and I were celebrating our success when I got a phone call from Anita. She told me, hardly able to get the words out, that my brother had killed himself. I went into shock. When I told our set designer, he burst into tears but I felt little or nothing. I couldn't think straight. On the morning of my return home to London, I was in such a state, I nearly set my apartment on fire. Over the months, as my grief and anger began to surface, I began to feel I could write something, but not about my brother. It was just too painful.

Not long after this, I was asked to direct a play about Pushkin, the Russian poet. This proved to be the crucial turning point. The playwright and I were working through the script. I knew the play needed to be changed and I also knew that after the first round of alterations, the playwright didn't want to change it further. "This is the final version!" she told me definitively a few weeks before rehearsals began. "No more rewrites!" Now I had once rewritten another writer's play and I had gotten away with it. I'd improved it. It got good reviews, but I didn't win myself any friends for what I did. Directors rewriting playwrights' work – for better or worse – is not that unusual. But it's not widely advertised, and definitely frowned upon.

Of course when the playwright's dead, you can do whatever you want. I've actually re-written Shakespeare. Talk about hubris! I had to shorten *The Winter's Tale* so it could be done by students and I had to produce a bit of mock Shakespearean doggerel to cover over the scenes that I had excised. But when I was doing this kind of (re)writing I was really hiding. And one of the things I had to learn, if I wanted to write, was that I had to stop doing that.

So I was working on this play about Pushkin. We're not so familiar with his work in the English speaking world, but in Russia he's virtually the national poet – the Russian Shakespeare. A contemporary of our own Edgar Allen Poe, Pushkin was a hugely prolific writer. A novelist, a playwright and author of many wonderful fairytales. The opera *Boris Godunov* is based on a Pushkin story and *Eugene Onegin*, one of Tchaikovsky's most well-known operas, is based on a Pushkin play. Pushkin himself is a wonderful subject for drama. He was a genius, a rebel, a womanizer, a gambler, and a rogue. Always in trouble with the Czar, his creditors, the official censor and the Russian secret police, he was eventually killed in a duel by a rival for his wife's affections.

The playwright had taken Pushkin's most famous short story *The Queen of Spades*, adapted it wonderfully for the stage and woven it into the fabric of Pushkin's turbulent life – a concept I really liked. So what was the problem?

Her adaptation of the short story itself was brilliant. It was compelling, terse, dramatic, charged. But some of the scenes she'd written about Pushkin's life leading up to the story and after it were weak. Despite her reluctance to make changes, I knew she'd feel differently once we began to put the show on its feet. We'd worked together before. I liked her. She respected me. We got along well. And so rehearsals began.

Now you have to know that the director in the theatre doesn't have the power that the director has in the movies.

Especially in England where the playwright's work is sacred. So I'm in England in the middle of rehearsals for this show and I can see it's not working. We're on course to lose the audience's attention somewhere in the early middle of the play. Audiences have needs that you must meet if you expect to excite and hold their attention. Despite what novice playwrights may think, the actors can't do it all by themselves. As a director, when I exhaust every trick I know and it's still not working, I figure it's the scene. There's something wrong with the writing – and only the writer can fix that.

Now it's a week before the show is to open and I'm beginning to panic. The playwright has already made a number of crucial changes throughout rehearsals, but more are needed. So I go home and rewrite three critical scenes myself. And I come back the next day, sit down with the playwright and say, "Look, you're not gonna like this, but I've rewritten three of your scenes. The dialogue I've written is terrible, and I don't care if you keep it or not. It belongs to you now, but you have to fix the dynamics of the scenes so that something happens to move us forward towards the climax of the play." (Remember Aristotle saying a drama is a single action.) As she originally wrote it, the characters spent about 20% of their time on stage playing cards and making witty remarks. The dialogue was well written, but it wasn't serving the story. Think about this for a moment.

Our hero is on the verge of bankruptcy. His marriage is on the rocks. He's about to be killed in a duel. There's lots at stake, but the writer is not taking advantage of it. We're losing our audience through chitchat. And I'm not talking about Chekhovian chitchat. When Chekhov's characters chitchat with each other, the stage is alive with passionate subtext. In plays by Oscar Wilde, the master of banter and chitchat, every witty remark supports the character's aims and reveals his or her character. But here, the chitchat was simply that. Chitchat. And it wasn't going to hold the audience.

So I said, "You've got to find a way to make that chitchat work for the drama underneath." And to her credit, she did. She saw what I was getting at in terms of structure, reworked her material and solved the problem far better than I had. The play was a big success. On opening night, I'm sitting back feeling pretty pleased with myself because it's all going very well and suddenly I think, "I like it, but what if the critics don't?" My heart sinks. "If they think it stinks, the playwright gets the blame, which is unfair to her, but if they say it's good, I don't get any credit! I'm losing both ways." So I thought to myself, "This is not right."

In the end, the critics praised my directing. They had no idea of the difference my writing had made. But why should they? I'd used the playwright – who had the guts to stand up and be counted – to hide behind. This was a hard lesson and there was only one way I could fix it. Stop hiding.

When you write for the theatre you're right up against the audience. There is nowhere to hide. They are present with your work. The theatre is a great revealer for a writer because if you can't keep them turning the pages, as it were, you can feel them drift away. It's a visceral thing. If they drift off far enough, they may leave the room. The big question is always "how do you keep the audience attentive? How do you make them care? How do you manage their expectations and pay them off?"

Now, as a playwright and writing coach I am very, very conscious of this. Your audience wants to turn the page. They didn't buy your book to be bored. You have to take care of them. Unconsciously your readers will always be asking themselves: "Do I care about that character?" "Do I care about that idea"? If they don't, they'll stop reading. Part of your job is to make them care. That's what I did. Even though my words themselves were never used, my writing had made a crucial difference and this gave me the confidence to take a risk and begin writing for myself.

The Herald

The **Crisis of Disruption** is the event that knocks heroes out of their ordinary lives. It's the **Call to Adventure** or **Inciting Incident** that sets the Quest in motion.

The Crisis of Disruption

So this was my "Crisis of Disruption," and it's the first of the four crises I'll talk about today. My wife calls it "the inspiration phase," but for me inspiration didn't come out of the blue, it came out of the challenge of making someone else's play work. And if you think about any piece of writing that you do, the first thing that gets you moving is your inspiration. You get this idea and it seems to lead to something else, and grows stronger, kind of like a nibble on the end of a fisherman's line. But what about you, here in this room? What has inspired you?

> Lots of things, but often pictures start coming into my head and that's when writing starts to happen because these pictures are created.

Great! Yes?

> I saw a great tragedy take place, a great injustice. And I knew it was wrong. And I was inspired, I just couldn't stop writing about it.

That's beautiful. And I just want to say it again – "I couldn't stop writing about it." That's so typical of the inspirational state. "I couldn't stop writing about it." Yes?

> When I'm tired and I get in that recliner after a hard day's work, stories just come right into my mind.

Great! When she's tired she lies in a recliner at the end of a hard day's work, the stories come into her mind. Sometimes complete in themselves. That once happened to me. I just took dictation!

Yeah, yeah.

It was wild! Yes?

I can smell the smells and tastes the tastes.

She can smell the smells and tastes the tastes. Yes?

For me it's a character. A character will kind of fully form and the story will just flow after.

So for you a character will emerge. Okay. Let's hear some more.

For me it's an event. I was attacked by a moose! (Laughter) It may sound funny when I say it, but moose are huge, seven feet at the shoulder. They can weigh up to ¾ of a ton. If they get riled up, they can run you over like a truck. You don't want to mess with one of them. Writing it out helped me deal with it.

So sometimes the inspiration is… Well, you write because it helps you deal with a trauma. This is what happened to me after my brother died. You write because there's nothing else you can do. Yes?

There was a website that dealt with an area where I was the preeminent expert. They had a huge demand. About a half a billion hits in a three-week period...

Were you the expert on this website?

No. But it was my field.

So you thought, "this is something I can write about!" And for all of those of you who didn't see it, he made the dollar sign! Yes?

Surviving repeated misadventures.

Surviving repeated misadventures. And finally what then happens?

My son died in an avalanche. His body was buried in the snow for ninety-one days. That's the last thing that happened.

Right. Does that cause you to then want to write about it?

Well, I have wanted to write forever but this was the icing on the cake.

And did you then pick up the pen?

I have been doing it now, yes.

Good! Good. Because picking up the pen is the hardest thing, but it's also the most important. If you don't pick up the pen, you can't do anything. Here's a little story. Daley Thompson is a British Olympic champion. In one interview he gave to the BBC in the mid 1990's, the interviewer asked, "What is the hardest part of your training regime?" And he replied, "Getting out of bed in the morning." And if 'getting out of bed' is the hardest part of a champion's training, then 'picking up the pen' is the equivalent for a writer. It's the hardest thing. And it's hard because inspiration is disruptive by nature. It calls us to change, and change is scary, even when it's change for the better. Campbell calls this phase "The Call to Adventure" and, in the classic story, it's always followed by "Refusal of the Call." Taken together they form what I call, "The Crisis of Disruption."

Refusal of the Call

If you are reluctant to pick up the pen, or if you find it hard to follow your inspiration, guess what? You are not alone. There are hundreds of millions of human beings who, in one way or another, refuse the call. It's the rare hero in myths and stories that doesn't. Even when the hero is willing, someone in the story will be upset and perform that 'Refusal' function for them. Vladimir Propp, a Russian scholar of fairy tales who studied the 'shape' of folktales and who inspired both Campbell and Vogler, noted that story functions are often carried by more than one individual character. They are often shared between characters. So in Jack and the Beanstalk for example, even though Jack functions as the hero, it's his mother who refuses the call. She carries out the function of 'refusal' in the story when she throws away the magic beans.

The first Crisis of Authorship is the Crisis of Inspiration. In the context of leadership, I call it the Crisis of Disruption because it's the leader's job to interrupt "business as usual," to wake people up and get them to change. In doing this, the leader is enacting the archetypal story function of The Herald, the character or inciting incident in the story that calls the hero to adventure. And what is the inevitable response? According to Campbell and Vogler, The Hero or someone close to him will refuse the call, or resist taking action. The same thing happens to us as writers. Something in us refuses the call. First something in us is inspired. We start writing. Then what happens? Anybody? Come on fess-up. Does anybody just write on till the story is complete?

Sure, you have to.

Right. So you've finished. Including the 'second act'?

And the third.

And the third? Wow. Fantastic! You must tell me how you do that. For a lot of us, at the very least, we write until our inspiration runs out. But the story may not be finished. I have a play I've been working on for ten years – no, longer. Twenty years. My original inspiration is long gone! I've written probably 1000 pages of material. Now a play has to be no more than 100 pages, maybe 120 for a very long one. Absolute maximum, nowadays at least. So I've written a lot of stuff, I'm still wrestling with it. The challenge is when you leave the inspiration phase, what happens? Yes?

> When I think it's sounding good, I give it to someone to read. Someone I can talk to. Like my granddaughter.

And what do they say?

> Oh they say it's wonderful! (Laughter)

Great. And do any publishers agree?

> I don't know. I'm still working on that!

Okay. There's a couple more people who want to speak. Yes? You have a thought about this?

> I want to go back to your original question. You asked, when your inspiration stops, what do you do?

Yes.

I think when your inspiration stops, you should stop, too. You should stop for a while. Take a breath and review what you've done. Go over what you've written and wait until your inspiration comes back.

Good. OK. What tells you that? What tells you to do that?

*What do you mean? What tells me to **STOP** writing?*

Yeah.

My brain's done, I guess... I don't really know.

Okay. "My brain's done." What else? Yes?

What stops me is that I start to edit my work virtually the moment I've written it. Because I have a tendency to allow myself to just download and then I start re-writing right away. So I'm better to walk away for a while and then come back and look at it because I'll have some perspective.

Yes, absolutely, but what tells you to walk away and leave it alone?

Frustration. Confusion. You start to lose your original thought, you start to second-guess yourself.

Okay, but what tells you you're frustrated and/or confused?

You're sort of second-guessing. And so you seem to go off track or off-line.

Okay, okay. Yes?

> *It seems to me that the characters are in different stages. In the second act, a lot of writers go through their own second act. They're going through their own struggles with the work.*

I agree strongly. My wife says this about second acts. "You thought you were writing a story about a character that was outside of you. It turns out that the more and more you write, the more you meet yourself. And that the problems your character is having are the problems that you are having." I agree. Second acts are notoriously difficult because in second acts people get lost. The writers along with their heroes. Yes?

> *When I come to a stop, I ask myself the question, "So what?" "So what?" And then when I can answer that "so what" question, it gets me going again.*

That's a great thought. But I'm sure you can tell I'm fishing for something and we're almost there, so I may as well say it. What I'm hoping someone will say is… Yes?

> *You're looking for someone to say that they're blocked. Is that what you're saying?*

Not quite blocked but what do you do when inspiration runs out? Do you give up? Do you press on? How do you decide what to do next or even if it's worth going on at all?

The Mentor

The **Crisis of Direction** is the moment in the story where Heroes meet a Mentor to advise and guide them on their journey and help them handle their fear of the Unknown.

The Crisis of Direction

This is the Crisis of Direction. The moment when you need to find some new energy to give you guidance, support, or a kick up the backside. A Mentor to help you move beyond your fears.

In my case the important part of the process is getting it all out onto the paper. Getting through the first draft and actually saying to myself, "This is my first draft. It's mangy. It's messy. But it's my own!" Now we're going to hear a talk later today about actually trying to make it messy because it's supposed to be! This is a lot harder than it looks. We read our favorite novel and we think, "My God, how do they do that? I could never do something as wonderful as that!" What we don't realize is that it took the author years and the first draft was probably a train wreck, except for occasional bits and pieces.

Henrik Ibsen, the great nineteenth century playwright, used to say that his first drafts were always dreadful. And then he took himself through a very particular 'mentoring' process. He described it in this way. He took a long train journey with his characters. And had dialogues with them. And then they told him what was wrong. And then he went back and fixed things. That was his Mentor energy, his

Inner Mentor at work. Now this man had an unparalleled sense of dramatic structure. His plays, after *Peer Gynt*, are almost paragons of first, second and third act structure, even though some of them have four or even five acts technically. But he couldn't have done it without some internal source of wisdom. Yes?

> *I had a friend who told me "when the inspiration runs out, you need to have some faces looking at you and saying 'where is the rest of this? I want it!'"*

Yes, and this is one of the functions of The Mentor. To encourage you. Anita started a creativity group when we first moved to Palm Springs from London. Ostensibly she started the group to keep me from getting too depressed as we eased into 'retirement.' She called it The Mentor Group. The idea behind it was, "How do you help people take the next step in their current creative project?" And what we discovered was that support is far more important than criticism. At least at first. If a group is only about critiques or improvement it's likely to kill most work before it's even born. Because we all know we can't tell if what we've written is any good or not until weeks after we've written it. I go back and read my own work sometimes and I think, "Wow, that was good. I thought it was terrible when I wrote it." Or sometimes I write something and think, "Man, this is great!" And then I go back and read it later and think, "Ugh! Who wrote this crap?" My view is that you need Mentors who are going to help you because you're not even beginning to get to the place where things get rough. Not in my view. According to the myth, you're still in the ordinary world. We've been talking about how easy it is to get lost in the second act, but this isn't really the second act yet. It's just a foretaste of it. When you meet The Mentor you're probably still in the first act of your journey. Yes?

I'm sorry, but I've had this in my head for a while, so maybe I shouldn't...

No please, say.

Well it seems to me that when you were talking about inspiration, when people were talking about what inspired them, it was things that touched their souls. And we get so caught up with everyday living sometimes that we don't really listen to those things.

I think what you're saying is so important that I'm going to repeat it, so everyone can hear it. She said, "When you get caught up in everyday living, you often lose contact with the inspiration that touched your soul."

Yes. But I'm saying more than that. If, when you get into the writing, or you get writers block or whatever, if you can just get yourself back into that mode where

your soul was touched, you know, maybe that can
bring you back.

Yes! That's your own Inner Mentor speaking and it's wonderful advice. I'm going to take it myself! And it's perfect that you've brought it up right now because it shows us that this mythic pattern, this paradigm exists intrinsically – we already know it. Because there is some intrinsic part of us that has the wisdom to know what to do when inspiration is not enough. In the classic Western film *High Noon*, Gary Cooper does not have a living Mentor, or an Obi-Wan, to help him decide what to do. But he has a Code, a set of values. And his Code says, "You don't leave the town undefended – even at the risk of your own life." That's his Code of Honor. Right? I'm going to hold up *High Noon* as a good example later on because it will also give us an illuminating example of the final crisis, which I call The Crisis of Sacrifice. I want to move us on now, but before we do, let's take a look back at the ground we've covered.

The Story So Far

We've talked about the Crisis of Disruption: the Inspiration Phase. That's the first crisis.

Then we talked about the Crisis of Direction, that phase of your journey when your inspiration runs out. That's the second crisis. This is the place where you seek a Mentor on your writing journey to help you overcome your refusals or discouragements. You'll meet this crisis when you have written your first draft, or when you've become blocked, or simply lost your inspiration amid the distractions of everyday life. To help you through it, you seek out some-one – or some energy within yourself – to get back in touch with the sources that got you going in the first place. This is the moment when you realize that you can do this, if you really dig deep.

This is the moment in the film when the six-year-old boy is flying the 747, and he's in way over his head but then he says to himself, "I can do this!" I'm actually thinking of one of the incarnations of the *Airplane* movies, I forget which one. And it wasn't a six-year-old boy but it was the hero's old flame, the stewardess. She's on the radio to the tower at the airfield, and she's got to land this gigantic air-plane and she says to herself, "I can do this!"

That's the Crisis of Direction. Once you're through it, you know what you need to do to see it through. But of course, you still need to do it! So now we arrive at...

The Hero

The **Crisis of Commitment** is the point of no return. It's the moment in the story when heroes become **Heroes.** When they vow to see things through, no matter what the cost.

The Crisis of Commitment

This is the third crisis. In the first crisis you've been a Herald to yourself. You have called yourself to adventure or been inspired by someone or something. In the second crisis, you have found a Mentor, inner or outer, to help you move on, who has encouraged you, or trained you to take the next step, to push through the block. Now the question is, will you do it? Will you commit yourself fully? Are you really going to see this project through to the end, no matter what?

I've heard it said that all writing is rewriting. Only the greatest geniuses get it right first time (and we don't know for sure about them!) Ben Johnson said of Shakespeare that he never crossed out a line. Well maybe, because how else could you write thirty-six plays in ten years, virtually all of the masterpieces? You would have to be mainlining something. But I don't think it was quite like that, even for him, and it certainly is not like that for the rest of us.

When The Crisis of Commitment hits, it's as if the hero, Luke for example, has no other choice. Luke discovers that his uncle and aunt have been killed. Their house, his home, has been burned to the ground. His known world is in ashes. What is there left to lose? He's lost his last foothold in the way things were, so he makes the commitment to move forward into the future, into the special world (and save the Universe). The Crisis of Commitment is fraught with risk because you don't really know what you're getting into. You are committing yourself to the Unknown. And for you, too. When you write or create anything, you're stepping beyond what you know. I wish it wasn't the case – I really do. I wish I knew what I was doing – but I don't. In writing, you just have to take the risk. Even when you use a solid outline, the Unexpected will come and bite you in the backside – or at least you hope it does!

Now some of us are blessed, or perhaps cursed, with a special gift that makes this kind of commitment a bit easier to make. For example, I have an instinct for performing. I find acting really easy. I can still memorize pages of a character's lines without too much trouble, even though in other respects my memory is fraying pretty badly and I'm continually losing my keys, or glasses or cell phone. Also, I enjoy being in front of people even when I don't know what I'm going to say next. And I have a gift for performing in public even though I've never been a professional actor and never had to make my living at it. As a director too, I haven't suffered the intensity of the crises that I suffer as a writer. But writing is very close to me, it comes from an intimate place, even when I'm just trying to make a factual point or create a logical argument. So when I sit down to write, I have to somehow summon the energy of The Hero. And in my work with organizations and change – which is where the Four Crises model came from – there is always a time when leaders too have to behave like heroes; they can't just issue commands from afar, or advise or inspire. They have to be more than Heralds or Mentors. They have to act. They have to confront the opposition. They have to assume the role of the Hero. If they don't, no matter how much the troops are in agreement – if the general isn't willing to get his or her hands dirty or 'ride into the breach' – no one is going to follow. It just feels too unsafe.

The Big Unknown

Whenever you write from the heart, you are crossing into unknown territory. And you don't know whether you're going to be able to use the material that comes out of that place or not. You just have to stop hiding behind your gift, whatever it may be. Whatever it is that makes you feel in control. Your gift for language, or dialogue, or character or anything else that makes your writing "good" and take the risk – like any hero. And take that leap into the empty page. Yes. It's awful.

There was a particular scene in the Pushkin play I spoke of earlier that I really loved. In it, Pushkin, the writer confronts the hero of the very story he's writing, because the hero won't behave as Pushkin thinks he should! And this is something all writers face in one way or another. Good writing is a balance between Artifice and Truth. No one wants to hear everything that goes on inside your head, but when something comes out that is authentic and true, it grabs you. It makes its own kind of sense. It's your authentic voice and, if you're like me, you know when you're writing from that voice and when you're not. Now the challenge is, this voice might be authentic but it might not be doing what you need it to. For example, in the play I'm currently working on, I've got two characters that just won't behave and serve the plot! And when I tell them what I need them to do, they die. They lose their energy. They go, "Okay, I surrender. I'll do whatever you want – but you're not going to like it." I sometimes feel that when I'm not looking, they roll their eyes and shake their heads and wonder "who hired this idiot?" It's a very tricky proposition, this.

As a writer you can have "peak experiences," moments when YOU disappear, and WHAT'S WRITING – writes. It's the state of "flow" and it's wonderful, as if you were taking dictation from the Creative Mind itself! But the painful part is that sometimes, no matter how great this authentic voice is, you can't use it! There is a well-known agent and editor in New York named Noah Lukeman. (He also went to Brandeis, the same college I did, but many years later.) In one of his books on writing called *The Plot Thickens*, he confesses that, as an editor, he'd had to cut some of the most beautiful pages of writing he'd ever read. Only he and the author would ever know how good that writing was. Why did he cut it? Because, great as it was, it didn't belong in the book the writer had actually written. And this brings us, in a rather roundabout way to crisis number four.

In the traditional mythic story, when the hero has wrestled with the Dragon – let's take Beowulf as an example – Beowulf fights the monster, Grendel. Beowulf, strongman that he is, slays Grendel in that marvelous Scandinavian alliterative verse. And so everyone lives happily ever after. Right?

Wrong. Because if Beowulf thought Grendel was bad, Grendel's mother, who shows up to avenge her son, is going to be much worse. So in Act III, The Shadow comes back big time. Heroes, thinking they've defeated their enemy in the second act, seize their reward and set out, elixir in hand, back to their Ordinary World. But the fight is not over. Not until they become a different person altogether.

CRISIS OF TRANSFORMATION

The Shadow

The **Crisis of Transformation** is the ultimate moment of truth. In order to defeat the Shadow, Heroes must sacrifice their old selves and change.

The Crisis of Transformation

Remember when I talked about Gary Cooper in *High Noon* and his Crisis of Direction, his encounter with his own inner code of honor? Does anybody remember in *High Noon* what part Grace Kelly plays? Yes. The wife. The film's story starts on the day she and Gary Cooper are married…

And she's Amish or…

Quaker. She doesn't believe in violence. Her principles say that you should never use violence to solve a conflict. And in the film when it becomes clear that Gary Cooper is going to stay and shoot it out with the outlaws, she leaves him. She says "if you're going to stay and fight these bad guys with guns, I'm leaving you on the noon train."

(Someone in the audience starts to sing) "Don't forsake me oh my darling…"

That's exactly right, "Don't forsake me oh my darling on this our wedding day." Marvelous. The film was directed by Fred Zimmerman and the script was written by Carl Foreman. It was adapted from the short story, *The Tin Star* by John Cunningham. So those of you who are short story writers, do not despair. You too can achieve greatness. You don't have to be a novelist to do it. There's a marvelous moment in this film. Does anybody remember in the third act what Grace Kelly does?

She kills one of them. She becomes The Hero.

Exactly. She becomes the hero. Why did she become the hero? What did she do?

She shoots the bad guy.

Yeah. In the back! Talk about breaking the code! First of all, a woman. Second of all, violating her principles. And shooting the bad guy in the back. What makes that film into a masterpiece in my view is that it's a tragedy in the brewing that's rescued in the last moment by a hero who goes into The Shadow for love. Because Gary Cooper's character cannot change. He's chained to his beliefs. The deck is heavily stacked against him, but he can't say to himself, "There's four bad guys against me. I can't find anybody in this godforsaken town to help me. The Towns-folk are so frightened they'd rather give in to the bad guys. The hell with this, I'm out of here!" But his code won't let him. Because he's Gary Cooper. And that's what you do when you're Gary Cooper. You stand and fight. And he's absolutely fantastic in that part. Absolutely deadpan. All of that feeling contained in a superficially expressionless face, but there's so much going on under the surface and in his eyes. So in order to save her husband, his wife has to go into The Shadow. She is the one who must change.

In the mythic story, in the final confrontation with the worst villain, the hero becomes like the very Shadow with whom he's in conflict. Heroes make a choice to do what is completely against who they are in order to prevail. Rick, in *Casablanca*, starts out as a cynic. "I don't stick my neck out for nobody," he says. And in the end he sticks his neck out for everybody. Scrooge is a miser who, in the end, sacrifices his character flaw and becomes generous. But what about Doctor Henry Jekyll in *Dr Jekyll and Mr. Hyde?* Henry Jekyll cannot bend. He cannot become like Mr. Hyde, so Mr. Hyde wins and kills them both. Jekyll is eternally split off from his opponent. He cannot be 'bad,' even for a moment and it kills him. That's another brilliant story.

But let me return for a moment to why I think *High Noon* is such a brilliantly constructed drama. Remember how I talked about how characters perform functions? In the third act Grace Kelly becomes the hero of the film. Why do I say this? Because the function of the Hero Archetype is threefold. First: to move the story forward. Well, Gary Cooper does do that for most of the picture.

Second: to serve and protect The Mentor's vision, which Gary Cooper also does – he serves his code. But the third function of the hero is to make the sacrifice that changes everything. And that he cannot do.

Grace Kelly's character is the one who changes. She sacrifices her beliefs for something more important. She resolves her dilemma between love and duty – her father would definitely not approve of her shooting someone in the back – by choosing love. She chooses to step beyond her own code, because Gary Cooper's character is stuck in his. But the real beauty of this is that when she changes, then Gary Cooper can change. You remember the fantastic last shot of that film. The last bad guy lays dead in the street. Gary Cooper and Grace Kelly are about to climb into the buck board and ride away. And Gary Cooper takes the Sheriff's badge, the tin star that's been pinned to his shirt throughout the film and, with great disdain, throws it in the dust. His wife has made the sacrifice that allowed him to change and he finally is able to climb off his high horse and realize that there are limits to his code. If people are not willing to save themselves, they just might not be worth saving. (This was Foreman's coded message to his colleagues in Hollywood, who betrayed their friends before the House Committee on Un-American Activities in the 1950's by naming names.)

So How Does All This End?

In a Drama, if your hero has not undergone some form of change, or if someone or something has not performed the function of change, your audience will not be satisfied. That's the reason I call the work we're going to do tomorrow *Voices of the Change Journey.* Imagine, for example, that Luke had looked at the broken body of R2-D2 and said, "Oh gosh, I've lost my technology. I can't use the force!" Would we be satisfied? Of course not. Imagine if Scrooge had said, "I'm going to be the world's greatest miser and that's it, let Tiny Tim die. Who cares?" Would we have been satisfied? Absolutely not. If Rick, who changes so fantastically in *Casablanca* had not transformed, he could never have said to Ilsa, "The problems of two little people don't amount to a hill of beans in this crazy world." Would *Casablanca* ever have become the classic that it is? I doubt it. (I love that line by the way. And the Epstein brothers, who wrote the script, came up with it only three days before they shot it. They didn't have an ending till the very last moment.) So how does this affect you as an author? Well, now we get to the crucial question. How does all this end? Well I haven't gotten there yet, but my wife has. She's always ahead of me in everything and she's been working on a book for how long?

Eight years.

Eight years. It's a book of essays about religion and the feminine. Philosophical essays. Deeply researched, she spent a lot of time in museums, The British Library and the Institute of Oriental and African Studies in London, struggling to get this thing out. She'd say, "I'm gonna write it in a year. I'm gonna have it done." Every year it's "this year I'm going to finish it." At last, after eight years she came back and said, "It's going to have to be a completely different book than I thought it was going to be. I just can't do the thing I had in mind."

Now sometimes you hit it lucky. Noel Coward wrote *Blithe Spirit* (well three quarters of it at least) over a long weekend. Remember, he was a brilliant craftsmen. He had internalized the rules of dramatic structure over years of work – and even he had a little bit of a problem with the ending. Anyone who knows *Blithe Spirit* knows it's a very, very funny and brilliantly constructed play about a man who's haunted by the ghost of his first wife because she's jealous of his living wife. But working in that kind of inspirational state through to the end – like Coward was able to do – is pretty unusual. Most of the time the book you thought you were writing is not the one that you're really writing.

There's a great French film by François Truffaut called *Day for Night*. Does anyone know this film? It was released in the early 70's. Now Truffaut was a famous filmmaker in the 1960's. He was a leading light of the French New Wave that had such tremendous influence on the movies of the 60's and 70's in this country – indeed all over the world. *Day for Night* is a wonderfully enjoyable film about the filmmaking process. In it, Truffaut plays himself, a film director making a film. He is the narrator, as well. His character is continually solving problems, dealing with actors and crew and their affairs, traumas and dramas. And there's this unforgettable moment where he's reflecting on the filmmaking process.

He says to us in voiceover, and I'm paraphrasing here: "You know this film stinks. I feel this every time I make a movie. I start out convinced that this is going to be the greatest film I've ever made. This will be *IT*. And the further I get into making it, the worse it gets. And finally I go through a kind of dark night of the soul and think, 'This is terrible. I'll never finish this. The actors are dreadful. It's the worst thing I've ever done, just one failure after another. Everything is compromised.' Then, somehow there's a glimmer. I follow where this leads and, in the end, the film becomes what it's going to be – I'm just the last to know what that is."

The film itself has to throw him off its back.

If your work does this to you, my whole message to you here today is "you're not alone." There is a profound level in which you are not only telling the story, but you're in it, living it. I don't know if you remember, but there's a moment in *The Lord of the Rings* when Frodo and Sam are sitting on the hillside overlooking the Black Gate that leads into Mordor. Sam asks Frodo what people might say about them when their story is told, as if what was happening to them were a story and not real life. And in a way we, as writers, are living a story too… no, a story is living us.

Now this story we are living is not a perfect confirmation of the ideal, as Vogler stresses. The map is not the territory – it's only an approximation. Character functions and the acts of the story, as we'll see in more detail tomorrow, are more like motifs than rigid, eternal pathways. Sometimes stages are left out, or they appear in a different way. Sometimes the "Gary Cooper" character makes the sacrifice and changes and sometimes it's the "Grace Kelly" character that makes the change. The important thing is that the function still exists. Even in classical James Bond movies, where James Bond is cool as a cucumber all the time, something does change. Usually the bad guy dies. So there is some form of change that's realized. But if you look at what you've written, you'll often find your stories have done this on their own. They fulfill these functions without you consciously planning them. But today, my concern is not so much with the story itself. It's with you. And me.

When you are inspired, you may strike it lucky and your inspiration may take you right through to the end. (Or at least till you're well into the third act, like Noel Coward). But, if you're not so fortunate, then it's probably wise to find a Mentor. This could be a support group, your spouse, a teacher or anyone you trust. Someone to help you understand where you're going. But knowing that you'll never know for sure until you get there. Sometimes you write something you think is going to be a comedy and it turns out you're writing a tragedy. There's a famous story about the play *Arsenic and Old Lace*. The playwright intended it to be a drama. It turned out to be a macabre, screwball comedy. Another example is George S. Kaufman and Moss Hart, in their first collaboration together.

Moss Hart tells this story in his memoir, *Act One*. They had just written this marvelous, sprawling three-hour play for Broadway. As was the custom of the day, they took it on out-of-town tryouts to cities all over the East Coast, places like Boston and Philadelphia before it opened on Broadway, to work out any problems with the production and improve the script. And they've got massive sets and have been working on it for months. George S Kaufman, who, in addition to being co-author is also directing the production. He is, at this time, the preeminent craftsman of the American stage with a glittering string of hits to his credit. One day, after a grueling night of rewrites, Kaufman turns to Moss Hart, his young collaborator, and says, "I'm sorry, we can't make this work. I've told the producer that we're junking it. We are walking away. The audience has been laughing for two acts and suddenly, in the third act, they want to leave. We're going to close the show before we get to Broadway and lose our shirts."

Now for Moss Hart, the young playwright who came to Kaufman with the idea, it was a huge disappointment. This was to be his big break. This was supposed to have made his fortune (and it did, because there is a happy ending to this story). What happened was a classic example of The Crisis of Sacrifice. Kaufman says to his young protégé, "Here's your last paycheck, go on back to Brooklyn to your coldwater flat – I wish you luck in your future endeavors." So Moss Hart goes home. But he can't get the play out of his mind. He thinks, "There's got to be a way to fix this. There's got to be a way!" Finally, he gets this idea. "We've got to junk the whole third act and get rid of this big production number and replace it with something more intimate and human." (That means they'd throw $25,000 worth of sets into the trashcan and in those days $25,000 was a huge sum of money.) So Hart goes from his third floor walk-up in Brooklyn to Kaufman's Fifth Avenue Penthouse overlooking Central Park. Imagine how Kaufman's feeling at this moment. He's had to abandon a major production. He's bet his reputation on this thing and he couldn't make it work. He doesn't really want to see Hart, but Hart insists. (Kaufman at that moment is playing cards with Groucho Marx!) Hart barges in and says, "We can fix the play, here is what we need to do…" Kaufman recognizes that he's right. So they start rehearsals.

In his book, Moss Hart describes this unforgettable moment when he walks up to the stage door just before opening, seeing the $25,000 set broken up and stuck in the trashcans in the alley behind the theatre. That was the sacrifice. They had to junk a scene they loved in order to make the play from a flop into a hit. The play is called *Once in a Lifetime*, a fabulous and funny play about Hollywood and the coming of "The Talkies." It's the story of three failed New York stage actors who decide to go to Hollywood to make their fortune by teaching silent movie actors how to talk. It's a beautiful satire on the Hollywood system, and, because I was raised in Hollywood – my Dad was a stage and film producer – I had strong feelings about the material. And I directed a production of the play way back in the 1980's, when I was working in London. It's one of my favorites. So now it's three minutes past my allotted time. I hope you've enjoyed this talk and learned something too, and I look forward to speaking with you again tomorrow.

The Crisis of Disruption

The Inspiration Phase, when some powerful incident or event – something you see, feel, hear or imagine – becomes a Herald that calls you to the adventure of writing.

The Crisis of Direction

When your inspiration runs out and critical voices assail you and urge you to turn back or give up, you need to find some source of wisdom, an inner or outer Mentor to help you recover your sense of direction and take the next step.

The Crisis of Commitment

When you know what to do, you still have to do it! At this moment you step into the Hero's shoes and commit to seeing your project through to the very end no matter what. The only thing you really know is that you must push on.

The Crisis of Transformation

In this last crisis, you confront the ultimate choice. Do you remain stuck in your grand ideas of what your book could have been? Or do you give them up and finish the book it has actually become?

Day Two

Living the Story

Living the Story

For those of you who expect another talk about The Four Crises, I'm done with you. We did you yesterday. We did the writers. Now let's do the story itself.

Today I'm going to take you on a voyage through the landscape of dramatic storytelling – and I mean that literally, as you'll see. It would be wrong of me to contend that the dramatic landscape that we're going to explore today is the only one that exists. There are various alternatives, particularly more modern ones, but this one, The Hero's Quest, is both ancient and universal. It goes something like this.

Heroes are catapulted into an adventure to set the world to rights. They struggle against an Antagonist or Shadow and are almost overcome when, in the nick of time, they discover something about themselves and/or the world that allows them to prevail. There is something here that is so fundamental to the way we think, that a young child, without any level of sophistication or learning, will understand it as a story.

In 1995 I devised and directed a long-form improvisational theatre piece for a children's theatre in Sweden. We called it *In the Story Factory*. And, every day the actors would improvise a new, original story from beginning to end. We explored various ways to do this. Most often the story ended with a hero or heroine fighting some demon king or bad guy or bad witch and slaying it. But I told the actors, "When it's your turn to be the villain, don't die too easily please." I did this to keep the stories from becoming the same, day after day, and I also wanted the actors playing the heroes to be more inventive. One day, our hero, who happened to be a young woman, killed the Demon King. In triumph she turned her back on his slaughtered corpse, and all the kids were cheering. And then, to everyone's surprise, The Demon King slowly rose again! There was a sharp intake of breath in the audience and I heard a little voice pipe up, "that wasn't supposed to happen!" Now how did she know that? From a screenwriting seminar for 9 year olds perhaps? Of course not. There's something incredibly organic, even inborn in us that tells us what should happen in a story.

How Stories Work

So how do stories work? There is a brilliant innovator and improvisation teacher named Keith Johnstone who wrote a book called *Impro*. A marvelous and very funny book, beautifully written with lots of examples, games and exercises. Johnstone has also written a second book called *Impro for Storytellers* – equally as fascinating. He says that a story is, at its root, the account of a hero or central character going about routine, everyday actions that suddenly get interrupted. The hero struggles to reestablish the routine, but by the time he or she has finally managed to accomplish this, some kind of irrevocable change has taken place. The world of the original routine is never the same. Let's try one right now.

"Every week, Johnny went to the store for his mother. He did this during the winter. He did it during the spring." Now what are we waiting for?

Something different.

Yes. Something different. So, "One day, he went to the store…" And?

Got hit by a bus.

"Got hit by a bus!" (The audience laughs.) That's what improvisers would call a 'Block' because it's pretty much ends the story. (Lots more laughter) But maybe not! Let's keep going. "He got hit by a bus and…"

…lost his memory.

Yes! Great! "And lost his memory. He picked himself up and looked around and… began wandering." Now look at yourselves. 90% of the people in this room are on the edge of their seats wondering…

What happens next?

Yes. 'What happens next?' And why? Because we established a routine, then we broke it, which raised our curiosity. Then, one of you pulled our fat out of the fire by suggesting the bus had not killed Johnny, but simply caused him to "lose his memory" and thus the adventure begins and we are fascinated. So how do we pay off that fascination? Keith Johnstone says that after a while, an improviser should reincorporate something that they've already said by accident into the ongoing story. The bus might show up. The store might show up – because that's where he was going in the first place. Johnny's mother might show up. When you do this kind of 'reincorporation' as an improviser you give the audience a feeling that you actually know what you're doing. You don't of course, but in the audience's mind there is a feeling that it must be meant. The great playwright Anton Chekhov said the same thing. He said if you show the audience a gun over the mantelpiece in Act II, you've got to have somebody use it in Act IV. You have to pay off the expectation you've raised. Improvisers build a platform. That is to say a set of routine actions. For example, in a supermarket people are buying, and checking out food. Going through the aisles and all the rest of it. Then, according to Johnstone, you tilt the platform. Somebody or something changes and things go out of balance. And skilled improvisers will allow themselves to be changed, thus they move the story forward. Good improvisers learn to allow change to happen, unlike most of us!

In real life, most of us don't want to be changed. Even when we're miserable, we don't really want to be changed. We like it the way it is. And in the classic story, almost as if to reflect this, whenever the Herald calls the hero to adventure, the hero almost always refuses the call.

First Act Decisions

In *Casablanca*, Bogart says, "Of all the gin joints in all the towns in all the world, and she has to walk into mine." Do you think he wanted Ingrid Bergman – the girl that hurt him so badly – to come walking into his saloon and turn his life upside down all over again? Do you think he wants to save the man she left him for?

When Obi-Wan give Luke his father's sword, he says, "This is your father's sword. Now Luke, all you have to do is use it to save the universe." And Luke says, "Are you nuts? I'm going back to the farm." And what happens when he goes back?

He finds it's been destroyed.

Yes. The farm has been destroyed. His uncle and his aunt have been killed. And he makes the decision, amid the ruins of his old home, to do what he first refused to do. He sets off with his father's light sabre, and his allies, to save the Universe.

Now I've segued from improvisational storytelling, into the larger landscape of the three act drama. This is the landscape we're going to explore today. We've just been looking at what is traditionally speaking the space of The

First Act. The First Act challenges the hero to make a decision. To leave his or her ordinary world and cross a threshold into the unknown, into the special world of Act Two. It does this by breaking the hero's routine. In *Casablanca*, the music is playing, Bogart, who hasn't taken a drink in years, is sitting there getting drunk and he makes up his mind to win back Ingrid Bergman, even though she's married to the greatest freedom fighter who ever lived. So that's how Rick is going to get into trouble, into unknown territory. That's the end of act one in *Casablanca*.

In *Star Wars*, Act One ends when Luke makes the decision to join with Obi-Wan.

Second Act Complications

What's the next scene in *Star Wars*? Does anyone remember?

He's in the car.

Yes. Luke, Obi-Wan and the robots are in that floating car. And they pull up to the town and Obi-Wan does a Jedi mind trick on the guard, and they all cross the threshold into Act Two. In passing, I will also say that Mentors often have special gifts they give to The Hero. The light saber was one. The training in the use of The Force was another. It's a gift that Luke refuses actually. He says, "I can't do it." Which is also typical. But Act Two signals the entry into the Special World. The world where the rules are different.

Next, they go into this bar, remember that incredible scene that looks like it's out of some bizarre Western? Usually in the second act, the hero gathers together allies, goes through some tests and eventually gets sucked into what Campbell called "The Belly of the Whale" which, in this particular instance, is The Empire's lethal killing machine, the Death Star. Luke and his team are captured but manage to escape and rescue the Princess. Luke survives a life and death battle with the beast of the garbage compactor, climbs out of his ordeal and R2-D2 signals that he has the plans the rebels need and now they all have to escape. They fight their way out to the landing bay and it looks like the story should be over now because they got what they set out for. They've got the plans. They've saved the Princess. And they've escaped in the Millennium Falcon. But is that the end of story? No.

In the second act, The Hero goes through what Campbell calls The Ordeal. In Luke's case, it's the battle with the Garbage Beast. Typical of this phase is that the Hero tastes death and there is a sacrifice. The Mentor often dies and if you remember Darth Vader kills Obi-Wan just after this. Obi-Wan's sacrifice allows the Millennium Falcon and our heroes to escape to freedom. Alarmed, one of the Empire's underlings says, "But Lord Vader, they are escaping!" "Don't worry," says Lord Vader, breathing heavily in that mask of his, "I've put a tracking device on them." So there's more to come. Act Three begins.

Third Act Consequences

So here they are, in Act Three, fleeing out of the Belly of the Whale, out of the Special World, back to a world they understand – but now pursued by The Antagonist. The motif that Lucas uses here has an ancient pedigree, it's called Magical Flight. The heroes, having got what they went for, awaken to the really bad news. Remember when Grendel is defeated in Beowulf? His Mother shows up. Things only get worse. The Ordeal was hard, but the story now catapults the hero and his allies into the third act where things get harder. Even when Heroes triumph—

It's a pyrrhic victory.

Yes, exactly. A Pyrrhic victory. The second act ends in what I call a provisional solution to the original problem. And in the third act, this provisional solution is going to be tested and either stand or fall. The third act is the act of Consequences.

- The First Act is the act of **Decision**.
- The Second Act is the act of **Confrontation.**
- The Third Act is the act of **Consequences**.

Sacrifice and Change

In the third act of *Casablanca*, if you'll remember, there's another Magical Flight. Rick steals a car and rushes Ilsa and Victor Lazlo to the airport with the Nazi Major Strasse in hot pursuit. "Follow zem! Follow zem!" Strasse screams in his German accent. Right? I wish I could do all the accents in that movie. I'd impersonate the whole cast – Bogart and Bergman and Peter Lorre, Sidney Greenstreet, Claude Rains, Conrad Veidt – the lot of them. I would do that entire movie. Dialog and mime – with background music too – if I could!

Anyway, in Act Three, the chickens come home to roost. This is the act where the hero shows what he or she is really made of. Something's got to give, and it's the Hero who's got to give it. This sacrifice brings about revelation and change. In *Star Wars* it's when Luke is forced to give up his reliance on R2-D2's technology and finally chooses to "Use the Force." This is the problem he's been wrestling with since he first met Obi-Wan. "Do I take up my father's Jedi legacy or not?" Drama is not just about conflict, it's about choosing, too. There's always a dilemma and a difficult choice to make, usually, as a result of a revelation or reversal. Heroes make that choice and it changes them and their world. That choice is not one they planned on making. Luke didn't plan on using the force. Rick didn't plan on giving up Ilsa. Scrooge didn't plan on being generous and saving Tiny Tim. This is the kind of change that lies at the heart of most dramatic stories.

So stories have a beginning, a middle and end. In the beginning, in the first act, the hero makes a decision to leave home. To leave what they know. Their routines have been interrupted enough and broken enough and tilted enough that they actually make the decision. So they make the big decision to step into the danger and risk of the second act. Once they do, things get more and more difficult. They face obstacles, deception, competition, betrayal, setback after setback until they appear to solve the problem, but it's not enough. The Shadow still challenges them until they make the sacrifice and change.

The Opposition Archetypes

There are many genre variations to this story, but I think you can always recognize pieces of it. The Call of The Herald can be telephones ringing, planes crashing into buildings, little holographic movies being projected from robots. In *Casablanca* it's when Peter Lorre gives Rick the letters of transit, just before he's captured by the police. "I'm shocked! Shocked to find there's gambling going on in this establishment!" cries Claude Rains as he drags Lorre off to jail and collects his winnings.

In addition to The Herald and The Mentor, who enable The Hero's forward movement, Act Two is fraught with archetypes that oppose the hero's progress. The denizens of the Special World: Threshold Guardians, Shape Shifters and The Shadow itself – the main antagonist.

Threshold Guardians

Threshold Guardians function to test the hero's ability, determination and resolve. They often appear early in the story as part of The Hero's refusal. Jack's mother is a Threshold Guardian. Do you remember in *The Wizard of Oz* when Dorothy's allies approach the lair of the wicked witch? They're wondering how they can possibly save her from such a well-guarded Fortress. Do you remember how they do it?

They dress up as the guards.

Yes. They dress up as the guards. This is a very common fairytale mechanism for getting past a Threshold Guardian. And not just fairy tales. When I first started out in business, I started wearing a suit. It turned me from an interloper into an insider. Suddenly people thought I knew what I was talking about. I looked like I was part of the gang.

Shape Shifters

The second antagonistic archetype is the Shape Shifter. Give me a classic Shape Shifter.

Werewolves? Vampires?

Vampires. Werewolves. People who betray.

'On the Waterfront.' The brother who fixed the fight.

Yes, that's a great example. People who mislead and betray. The function of the Shape Shifter is to confuse. They confuse the hero and his or her allies. Shape Shifters are kind of Anti-Mentors. As a young man I worked in a film production house in Boston, and there was a guy, an older guy. And he was very, very friendly and he continually gave me advice that got me into trouble. And I'd look back at him and he would raise his eyebrows and shrug as if to say, "You should've learned." He was a Shape Shifter. Organizations and political alliances are filled with shape shifting energy. In such situations the psychological pressures are so great that even quite good people become Shape Shifters to cover their asses and hedge their bets. In business, change committees and commissions are often set up to perform the same function – to disable rather than enable change.

The Shadow

This brings us to the final archetypal energy in stories, the source of antagonism and opposition that Joseph Campbell calls The Shadow. This Archetype is not so easy to explain completely so the simplest thing to say is that the Shadow functions as the opposition. There's quite a bit more to it, as I'll explain later, but for now it's enough to say that the goal of The Shadow is to destroy the hero's quest.

Now, we all have these archetypes within us, otherwise we couldn't recognize them. Campbell actually identified many more. The King, The Warrior and many others. But for me, in terms of how stories work – Herald, Mentor, Hero, Threshold Guardian, Shape Shifter, Shadow – these are enough to be getting on with. Beginning, Middle, End. The pattern of the story is actually just the way our lives work when we need to change. And now we're going to find out a little bit more about this, but not from me. You're going to discover that you know it already. All you have to do is dare to remember and I've got a game to help.

Change Dialogue

I call this game Change Dialogue. It's a theatre game and it derives from three sources: Voice Dialogue technique, The Hero's Journey and Western Zen. I've already talked a lot about The Hero's Journey, and I'll talk about the Zen influence in a minute, but first a word about Voice Dialogue.

Are there any other writers in this room who have an Inner Critic that sits on their shoulders and continually tells them what's wrong with them and how they should fix it? Okay, I see I'm not alone. This voice seems to have a life of its own, doesn't it? In my case, when it starts criticizing, it's pretty demoralizing and it feels punitive, but does it have to be that way? Could it be different? Maybe my Inner Critic is just my brain's way of telling me what's wrong so I can fix it! Maybe that's why this voice exists – so I'll get things right! And if that's true, then this voice might want to prepare me to face other people's criticism too, by getting in there first.

It's Preemptive.

Yes. Preemptive. It's possible that this voice may want me to do well, to be safe and to prosper – if we could just talk to each other. Now you could say that we contain a whole cast of voices like this – not just a Critic, but a Pleaser, an Achiever, a Rebel, an Artist, a Protector – about as many as you can think of. And each of these Inner Voices has a unique identity, a job they try to do for us, and an ongoing story to tell. They are the cast of 'selves' that make up the drama of who we are.

In the 1970's, psychologists Hal and Sidra Stone developed a unique way for people to enter into this drama and learn from it. They called it Voice Dialogue. It created a space for their clients to give voice to their disowned selves and, by speaking, to heal the inner conflicts that plagued them. Change became possible. Their clients became more aware, resourceful and effective in their lives.

Okay, so what has Zen got to do with this? Well, in the late 1990's, my Zen teacher, Genpo Merzel Roshi, developed an innovative use of Voice Dialogue he called the 'Big Mind' process. Originally created to make traditional Japanese Zen teaching more accessible to the Western mind, Genpo went from facilitating the internal voices of a single person, to accessing the collective, transpersonal voices of large groups like this one. His work was a revelation to me. (See the 'Acknowledgements' section at the end of the book for more details.) Genpo's innovations convinced me that we can enter into dialogue with – and learn from – anything we can imagine or perceive: a feeling, a concept, a quality, anything we have the courage to explore. Using tools from my work in organizational training, theatre and improv, I adapted Voice Dialogue to enable virtually any group to look at an issue or to think through a current challenge in a safe and productive way. To 'give voice' to unrevealed, unknown or unspoken aspects of a problem they face. I call it the 'Change Journey Process.'

We're over a hundred people here and as I facilitate this group, you'll have an opportunity to experience this for yourself. You'll find you know a lot more than you think you do and you'll be amazed by the innate wisdom of the people in this room – including yourself! Sound good? Ready?

Wow. Let's go for it!

All right, but before we begin, there are a couple of ground rules you need to know.

The first Voice I'm going to ask to speak to is called The Controller. I want The Controller to speak because I want you all to feel that you are in control of this process. Also that I'm not going to do anything weird. And your Controller will have the opportunity to speak if it wants to, or not to speak if it doesn't. It can participate silently, too. And this is important. When I ask for a voice, whether it's The Controller or any other, I want you to shift your physical position a little in your chair. This will help you interrupt the routine of your everyday self and move you to the place where a new voice can speak. Now don't worry about overthinking this, anywhere you move to is fine. Wherever you end up, you'll be in the right place. Don't ask me why this works. It just does. It's a mystery!

Now, rule number two. The game we're about to play is a theatre game. It asks you to play a role. In this case it's the role of someone (or something) other than your everyday self. Just let This Voice speak freely – even if you don't know what it should say. You can't really make a mistake. Honest! Remember the key word here is play. It's a game.

Just give it a try. Let the voice speak and it might surprise you with its wisdom. And I know it sounds a little crazy but if the voice wants to talk about you, let it talk about you in the third person – as if you were somebody else! No kidding. I think I can make this clearer by example.

If I am allowing My Controller to speak, it might have something to say about me. For example, it might say, from its perspective, "You know that Andy is just a handful. He never shows up to anything on time, I have to work like heck to get him some place, and I do. I work very hard - (laughter) You may think this is funny but..." And so forth. So I'll ask you to talk about your "self" in the third person, just like I did just now. That's the whole game.

To repeat, the two rules are: first, make a little shift in your physical position; second, if you speak about yourself, talk about you in the third person, as if you were someone else. I know it seems a bit odd to describe it beforehand, but don't worry, it will all make sense when we start. And when we get used to it, and your Controller is satisfied that everything is under control, then we can set out on our journey. The Controller, by the way, is the part of you that protects. You'll see. I don't want exactly to put words in your Controller's mouth but The Controller is called The Controller because it...

Controls things.

Exactly. Very good. All right we're already there! You know what to do already. So I would like everybody to make a little shift in position in their chairs and I'd like to speak to The Controller please. (*Sound of people moving in their chairs*) OK. So who am I speaking to?

The Controller.

Meet The Controller

The Controller. Great. Okay, so what's your job?

To control things. To keep Joanna safe.

To keep Joanna safe! Very good.

Not to be deceived.

Not to be deceived. Not to let her be deceived, right? Is she easily misled?

Yes, she is.

Yes, she is.

She's gullible.

Yes, she's gullible. And your job is to…?

To see through all the sham!

Yes, that's right! So you control things to keep her safe. Very good. Let's hear from more Controllers.

To keep her awake.

To keep her awake? (*Laughter*) Very good. Yeah, she's paid a lot of money to be here, you don't want her to fall asleep! (*More laughter*).

To judge others and Jonathan.

So you, as Controller, kind of judge others and Jonathan.

Yes.

What's Jonathan like? Is he a bit of a handful?

Yeah.

He gets out of hand?

Yeah, he's got a way to go.

Yeah. So you've got to keep him in line… Come on now, let the cat out of the bag, folks!

She's a mess. If I didn't keep her in control, she'd be an absolute mess.

Right! If you didn't do your job, which is to keep her in control, we don't know where she would be!

Nobody would.

In jail…? Or run over maybe? I mean when she crosses the street, who looks both ways? (*Laughter*) Is it the "self," walking along, head in the clouds, daydreaming, thinking about their novel? Hello! Who wakes the self up? Who does that job? It's you! The Controller. You keep him or her in control. Tell me more about yourself. Yes…?

I don't think you got my name right. I think I'm the director/dictator.

You know why I know I'm talking with The Controller now? You know why?

No.

Because you're even going to control the terms I'm using. (*Laughter*) Yeah! And I appreciate that. That's your job.

You're just being too nice.

I'm too nice? You think that I'm too nice? I want to know what The Controller thinks.

Maybe I should say Andy is too nice.

So The Controller thinks that Andy is too nice?

The Controller does think that Andy is really cool!

Well, I don't know about that.

> *She's not The Controller anymore. She's being 'THE SUCK UP' now! (More laughter. Another audience member speaks...) Will you just shut up and listen because he's got a lot of information that's useful so whatever I say I'm not going to know as much as he does.*

Okay, so you feel that whatever you say, or she would say or whatever other voices speak, you couldn't possibly know as much as this expert guy standing up in front of you here. Okay. He's flattered… I'm not. (*Laughter*)

> *I keep editing my Controller.*

Hold on… Could you repeat that please?

> *I keep editing my Controller. I'm trying to think of what to say but then I think "I shouldn't say that" and I keep editing myself.*

That's perfect. I *am* talking to the Controller. Because your job is to…?

> *Edit?*

Yes, to edit. That's perfect. Congratulations! You're doing your job!

> *I'm going to cry.*

Isn't it funny how we feel about the things that we do, when we feel we shouldn't be doing them? But it's your job, okay? And writers maybe don't appreciate us, as Controllers, because they think we just keep trying to mess things up. And, by the way it's perfectly natural to feel emotions during this process. Sometimes when these voices speak, they release strong feelings. It's perfect. It's great. OK, since I'm talking to The Controller now, tell me about the writer's struggle. You're right there with them on the firing line. Tell me about what it's like to be The Controller for a writer.

She's so wishy-washy.

The self is so wishy-washy. Yeah.

They can't make any decisions. And when they do, they just forget themselves, and I have to try and tell them and they don't listen...

Yeah. You're trying to help them out and they just can't make up their mind. Great. Very good. Let's have another one.

Empower.

To empower, great! Tell us about that. As Controller.

In the good way of control.

Well yeah! As The Controller, of course you are good!

Keeping them on the straight and narrow and...

Yes, that's your job! As Controller, the self might not like you very much, but it's your job to control things. As far as the self is concerned you keep her spontaneity crushed down. She thinks, "If I didn't have that damn Controller on my back, I'd be fine." But tell me, as Controllers now—

There are so many absurd, ridiculous notions going through her head, that it's all I can do to keep her from just bursting out with them... (Laughter.)

That's right! And in public!

Yes! And making an utter fool of herself.

That's right! That's right. And it's your job to keep her safe. Great.

How can this idiot spend the winter going to the gym working out, going cross country skiing and the first day he goes fishing, he smokes a pack of cigarettes! I could just shoot him. What's wrong with this guy?

I haven't got a clue. But I know how you feel. Andy is trying to lose weight but what does he do? Just stuffs his face all day long. He eats like there's no tomorrow. Yes...?

As the Controller, I purchased a manuscript review a little while ago and that should do it.

Good. That'll shut him up! (*Laughter.*) Very good.

Now I hated having to do it. But he needs the feedback.

Right. The writer needs the feedback.

Well, my writer gets on the Internet and gets in long arguments with other people on the Internet! And I can't get her to shut up.

And then she doesn't write.

Right!

She's just having an argument.

Why do some of these damn actors on TV, they don't even know how to spell things or say things, like 'Palm Spring' or 'phenomenas' you know?

Yeah, I do.

Or "a experiments."

Yeah. Can't they even learn a bit of grammar? That's right. Yes…?

I want to find a publisher first, and then write my book.

Write her book…

Yes, as The Controller I want to find a publisher first so the writer can then write her book.

Oh, right. Well I guess sometimes, Controllers, you can get a little out of control. And what is your biggest fear, Controllers?

Losing control.

Losing control. That's right. And when you're afraid that the 'self' is going to... what? Write some garbage? What do you do?

NIP IT IN THE BUD!

Yes! Nip it in the bud! 'She's not gonna write that!' 'He's not gonna write that!' 'I'll see to it!' Right. Okay. Now does the self appreciate you for this?

No.

Is this really what you want for the self? Now, come on, as Controllers do you really want to stop the writer from writing?

No.

No. Of course not. Now I want to move on to hear some other voices, but before I do, I would like to ask all The Controllers in this room something. If you had something to say to the self who writes, something that you feel would help you and your writer understand each other better, what would you say? This Change Journey process, by the way, on a psychological level is about reconciliation. But we can't reconcile if we don't speak the truth. So you've been absolutely marvelous in doing that.

I would say, "I'm just trying to protect you."

Right. That you are just trying to protect her. Not to…

I don't want to kill her.

Let's hear some more. Yes?

"It's okay to not be perfect."

It's okay to not be perfect. Wonderful.

"I really just want your best."

I want your best, but it's okay not to be perfect. Very good. What else?

"I don't want you to quit."

You don't want her to quit. Right. Right.

"Let's walk before we run."

Right. Let's walk before we run. Yes?

I don't want her to listen to me so often. I want her to go beyond the bounds more often, and not be so controlled.

So you would like to be a little bit more relaxed with her. So, what needs to happen between the two of you?

Trust.

Trust. Good.

Obedience.

Obedience. Well… you got a long way to go, gal! (*Laughter.*) "As long as she does what I say, there's no problem at all!" Okay.

I need some reconciliation.

Some reconciliation.

I need to translate everything for her because she has these thoughts but she does not know how to put them in the right words.

Right.

She can't figure it out. So I have to do a translation for her and spell it out.

Right. She can't figure it out. What would happen if you kind of just let her loose a little bit with the pen?

I don't know if she'd ever get it right.

Any other Controllers have a thought here?

She can always get her to go back and improve it.

All right, a few more.

I would say, "Jump and I won't let you fall."

Great. That's very good. So you would say "jump, I won't let you fall." Yes?

I would say, "all right, write all that silly stuff that you want to down, get it all out there and trust that later on you can go back and fix it."

Very good. Very good. So you would encourage her to write whatever is there and then come back to it.

To know that she's capable.

Great, so for her it's important to know that she's capable.

Yeah. It's important for her to know she can have fun.

So you would like to give her a little bit of courage to have fun! To have fun with her writing and not be so worried about you. Tell me this, do you have her best interests at heart?

Yes!

Of course you do. Yes?

There's a big difference between holding someone accountable, and holding someone capable.

Can you say a little more about that? As the Controller, and I'm speaking to the Controller now. *(Pause)* There is a difference, you say, between holding someone accountable and holding someone capable? (*Pause*) Do you mean, let me just try this out, do you mean that she, from your point of view she's capable and that... Say more.

> *Well, holding someone accountable means that you are in the upper position and the other person is in the lower position. But to hold someone capable means that you're on the same level. So it's a collaboration rather than an above and below thing.*

Wonderful! So, as Controller, you want her to know that you want to collaborate and not just be on an upper-level?

> *Yes. To collaborate.*

Right. Great. Fantastic! All right Controllers, you've been fantastic and those of you who I know have been quiet but listening, I know you've been there. The nice thing about this process is it works whether you speak or not. Even if you don't speak yourself, someone will say what you've been thinking. And just by listening you will learn more about who you are.

OK, we're about to go on a bit of an adventure. And I want to make sure you're ready, so I'm empowering you as Controllers, if you feel out of control during this process and you want to shut the process down for him or her that is fine. I'm not here to force you or to shame you, that won't work for anybody. I know your job is to protect and control things for the self. So when we go on this journey together, you decide if you'd like to let a voice speak or not. If you feel at all distressed or disturbed about anything, you just put up your hand and say, "I'm back"! (*Andy accidentally 'thumps' the microphone*).

Can we make that noise too?

Yeah, you can make that noise too! And you can say "I'm back, and I have this question!" or "I want to say this." Because without you, without your help Controllers, can the self create at all? If you deem it's unsafe to do so, would the self have access to his or her creative depths? Without your permission?

No.

No. You wouldn't allow it. So would it be fair to say that I need your help if we're going to speak to any other voices?

Yes.

Well that's what I'm asking you for. I'm asking for your help. And if you feel that it's wrong for the self, you can put your foot down. You are in charge now, not me. OK? Good. Could I ask you to make a little shift back to your everyday self for a moment? To your normal you? (*Noise of people shifting in their seats. Laughter.*)

The Ordinary Self

We'll all be normal now!

Can you feel the shift in the energy in the room?

It's lighter. Much, much lighter.

Yeah, because Controllers are in control – in their normal place – in the background, not in the spotlight. That's how they serve us, from behind the scenes. That's what they're there for. That's what they're hired to do. Now I'd like to ask, I'd just like to get your thoughts, the thoughts of your Ordinary Self. What was that like? To allow The Controller to take center stage and speak.

Intense.

Intense, yeah.

Relieving.

Relieving.

Grounding.

Grounding. What else?

Funny. Familiar. Empowering... Stressful.

Stressful. Yes. Could you say a little more about that?

When I see the actors talking on TV or whatever, then I'm thinking, "Dammit, what the hell, you know, why can't you get some frigging education!" You know that's stressful for me.

Right. Well it's very interesting, what we tend to do with these internal energies, these voices. I've asked to speak to your Ordinary Self because I think it would be useful at this point to share a bit of the theory behind Voice Dialogue with you, not just The Controller alone.

The Psychology of the Selves

We have two ways of behaving towards our internal energies. We could also think of them as voices or sub-personalities or patterns of behavior or patterns of thinking or 'selves.' The first way is that we identify with that self. It becomes part of who-we-are. Some people have incredibly strong and powerful identifications with The Controller, for example. "I'm cool under pressure. I keep control of things." Other people are different. When I was a hippie, I wanted to get rid of The Controller. It was, "Hey man, get off my back. I go with the flow!" So I identified with The Rebel. Now, if we identify with certain voices for long enough, they become a kind of mask. That mask is made up of those parts of us that we have learned to feel good about. The face we present to others – our socially-approved-of-self. Psychologist Carl Jung called this mask our Persona. Grace Kelly's Persona in *High Noon* is 'The Good Quaker Woman.' But what do you reckon we do with the energies we don't like too much?

Suppress them.

Yeah, suppress, repress them. Voice Dialogue says we disown that voice. We don't allow it to be part of us. Now this is a very interesting process for the drama, because heroes very often disown the parts that they don't like, but ultimately need to solve the dramatic problem. Think about Grace Kelly and what we talked about yesterday. She's getting married. Does she promise to "to love, honor, cherish and shoot people in the back for my husband?" No. That's the last thing she'll promise. She has disowned that aggressive side of herself. But, under the pressures of the drama – and to save her husband's life – she has to own it. She has to own that aggressive, violent part of herself. Jung called that part *The Shadow*. That's the place in our personality where all the disowned parts of us go. And Campbell's use of that term is no coincidence.

The Hero's journey *is* the journey into the Shadow to recover what's there. Rick, in *Casablanca* has disowned his idealism. He has to recover it. Scrooge is a miser; he has to become generous. The journey that we take ultimately moves us into the space where we meet the parts of ourselves that we really don't like very much. And your heroes – and heroines – will do the same. If they do take ownership of their shadow side, they learn and get bigger. If they don't, they don't change. They just go back to being their routine self. For Grace Kelly her routine was, "I'm a good person who's very nice and a Quaker who doesn't really get angry with anybody." But, when she breaks her routines and owns her Shadow-Self – BANG! Things change!

Now, we can have a voice dialogue conversation with anything we can conceive of. It doesn't have to be a 'personal' voice. So we can speak with any of the elements of drama. That's the beautiful thing here. And we're going to start now.

Controllers, I'd like you to give me permission please, I would like to speak to the voice of The First Act. So make a little shift, if you would Controllers, if you would allow it.

So who am I speaking to?

Call and Refusal

(The audience mumbles, hardly audible) - The first act.

Come on now, I can't hear you, who am I speaking to?

The Herald!

Okay. The Herald – in a way, yes. But now I'd like to speak to the voice of The First Act. Now Controllers I'd like you to make a space for the voice of The First Act to speak.

(Audience talks all at once.) The hero. The villain. The situation. The humdrum hero. My third grade teacher.

Okay. I need to back up. I'd like to speak to… I'd like to speak to all The Controllers in the room please. Controllers, I need your help now.

We need yours – for clarification. I don't know what voice you want?

OK. Thank you. Now Controllers, because I'm talking to The Controller now, aren't I? When you hear me say "I'd like to speak to the voice of The First Act," you don't know what I'm asking for, do you?

No.

Are you willing, Controllers, to allow the self to just take that risk? And just step into the unknown and say "First

Act here!" and find out who you are when we get there?
Are you willing? Controller?

Yes... No... Maybe...

All right, so thank you Controllers. You've done exactly
what I've asked you to do and that's great – you're protect-
ing the self. But, if you're willing to just let the unknown...
of course we don't know who that voice is or what it will
tell us, not yet anyway. This isn't a voice that the self has
usually been asked to speak from. I guess it seems a little
bit like me asking you to "let the voice of your shoe speak."
You must be thinking, "What? Are you crazy?"

(Laughter.)

Let's go on an adventure, I said it was going to be an adventure...

Just a minute please...

Yes?

> *You're talking about the major self that I am, so if I
> don't have My Controller on, then I'm opening myself
> up to vulnerability.*

You are right. Absolutely right. Beautifully put. Okay. So
Controllers, before we go on to speak with the voice of The
First Act, I'd like to take a little sidetrack. I'd like to speak

with another voice, if you would let me. I think this one will be pretty clear. Okay? I'd like to speak to the voice of Fear, please.

The Voice of Fear

Oh, I know that one.

Is that okay with you?

No.

That's good. If it's not okay, that's good too. You can just be quiet. You don't have to speak if it doesn't feel safe. You can just remain in Control and observe.

"What if I can't do it?" Is that the voice of FEAR? "What if I can't succeed?"

That's just fantastic, because that's who I'm speaking to right now, isn't it? Brilliant. This is wonderful! I am now speaking with the voice of Fear.

I'm FEAR! Get the hell out of the building! (Laughter.)

You sound like Anger to me. (Laughter.)

You're supposed to be afraid of Fear.

This is really interesting, so am I speaking to the voice of

Fear, or… yes?

> *Everything I have to say isn't really worthy, so I'm not really sure if I should say it, or write it, or if anyone would ever want to read it.*

Very good. Very good. So as the voice of Fear, you don't know if you really have a place. Yes?

> *I think you're being confusing, Andy. You're asking for a couple of different things. First, with Fear, there is a certain intensity, a certain intentionality. Are you asking to hear that? Or are you trying to hear the content of what one thinks about when they are afraid? It's hard to balance out because on the one hand, if you want intensity and emotionality then you'll get different kinds of responses. You'll get people who are being real quiet or you'll get some people who are afraid of the fall of a rock and some who are ready to fight. So the voice intonation will change, or the content of what they have to say will change depending upon how one reflects on that fear. So it's a...*

Well, you tell me. You tell me. When I ask to speak to…

> *I just told you. I'm telling you, the responsibility – (another audience member interrupts) I disagree. You sound more like The Controller... (then another...) He's analyzing too much...*

O.K. Let's take a breath. Now let's go back to the Story.

What does the Story say when the Hero is called to adventure? What do Heroes do?

They say, "I don't want to do it. I don't want to go."

Yes, Campbell tells us they refuse the call. They say, "I don't want to go." Now I've asked for the voice of Fear and what have I heard?

"I don't want to go."

Yes. "I don't want to go." "I'm frightened." "What do you want of me?" "I don't get what you're talking about!" Of course. That's Fear. And why does Fear arise? Because we're going into the Unknown. Now when you write, if you're going to write from yourself, where's it coming from? Where does genius and creativity come from?

The Unknown.

Yes. The Unknown.

The Void.

And what stops us from entering into that space?

Fear.

Yeah. Fear and loss of control. Fear! Wow! I can feel you now, man! I'm standing in front of this room and my throat is dry, my palms are sweating. I'm wondering if I should duck behind the podium here or if you guys are going to ride me out of town on a rail. (*Laughter*)

What if what I write is offensive to people.

Right. That's right. Now I'm speaking to the voice of Fear. So as Fear you feel, "What if what *she* writes is offensive to people?" *She* is the one who is writing, remember. Well of course she's worried about that.

What's going to happen if I tell the truth?

Yes. What's going to happen if she tells the truth?

People will be mad at her if she tells the truth.

That's right. People will be mad at her if she tells the truth.

What if she has no right to write it?

What if she has no right to write it.

What if she fails? And what if she succeeds?

That's right. What if she fails? That's bad. What if she succeeds? What's gonna happen?

If she succeeds, I go away.

If she succeeds, you, as Fear, go away.

I don't want to lose myself.

No. You don't want to lose yourself, do you? You want to be here.

But there will always be new things to fear!

Yeah, I have a feeling that there will always be plenty of things to worry about. Always plenty of things the self will be afraid of! I just have that feeling. Yes?

My Fear is not nervous at all.

As Fear?

No! I've been here before. I like being in charge. She needs to let me be in charge more often.

Okay! What is your function as Fear?

I don't know that I need a function. (Laughter.) I just get to sit in the easy chair and control things.

I think maybe I'm talking to The Controller a little bit.

I don't know. When The Controller was speaking it felt different. The Controller thinks. The Controller has nerves. The Controller has all these kind of nerves.

But you…

As Fear… Fear doesn't have nerves.

Yeah, Fear doesn't have nerves. You're just Fear.

I'm just a little more Elemental than that, really. I don't even have to think that much.

No?

No! I'm not thinking. I'm just sitting here enjoying my-self!

So what happens to her body when you're up...?

Oh, I don't care! (Big laughter.)

That's cool! All right, I get you. You're just Fear and that's it.

I'm just so Elemental that, you know... The Controller is the thinker. I'm just here. Since when is Fear about thinking?

Great point! So, as Fear, you're not about thinking.

No.

You're just about "I'm here." Too bad if you don't like it!

Right! Too bad for you.

Yeah.

I have my job to do - presumably. (Laughter.)

So what is the "presumable" job you do, do you reckon? I know thinking is not your strong suit. But -

Probably protection too. I know The Controller thinks that.

Yeah?

Yeah, fundamentally.

What I hear you saying is when you're in charge, you are in charge.

Right!

Okay, we've got at least three others who want to speak. Yes?

I can function as motivation.

Yes, absolutely right. You can function as motivation. Okay, yes?

I can hold her back.

As Fear, you can hold her back. Yes?

I can keep you alive!

Keep me alive? Or keep her alive?

Keep her alive.

Yeah, because without you, what's gonna happen?

She's gonna die. I make her faster and stronger.

Great. Very good. Very good. So as someone was saying… Yes?

*When whatever is coming at her is too big, I just slam
the door and run!*

Great. When it's too big, whatever is coming, the Unknown,
it's too big, so you slam the door. Very good. Yes?

*I'm the alarm bell. I just shriek as loud as I can so that
The Controller notices that something's going on and
can take care of it.*

Great. So you're like the alarm bell. So in a way… Yes?

*As Fear I've got a job to do and that job is to elicit a
decision because it's either fight or flight.*

Okay, very good. Very, very good. Yes?

*What if I write something that's not good enough? Or
what if I write something that's really, really good?*

Right, so as Fear you bring up "what will happen if it's
bad?"

Yeah.

Or "what will happen if it's really really good?" Because it's
about…

Success.

Right, you come up around the Unknown, don't you?

Yes.

Yes, you do. Now I'm going to summarize some of the things I've been hearing. As Fear, when you come up, you announce that a change is coming. Things are not going to stay exactly the same. So I have been talking to an aspect of the Herald but I've also been talking to an aspect of the Hero, who is terrified that the Call to Adventure is going to disrupt his or her life. We are, quite literally, living the story without even meaning to. We manifest these archetypal energies in ourselves without trying. I began by asking to speak to The First Act, and I actually ended up speaking to the crucial first steps of The First Act, even though it looked, for a time, like we went off on a tangent. It reminded me that in this human body is the story itself. We can't really get away from it. The Story is living in us, it's not something external to who we are.

Now I wonder if I can sneak something in here or if I'm just going to get into hot water.

Let's do it anyway. Come on, let's go. No fear!

All right there's the Call to Adventure. There's the Refusal and Fear – we've met them. Now, I'm asking all the selves in this room to allow me to speak with the voice of The Mentor. Okay? You happen to be the next step on the journey which is called "Meet The Mentor." Yes?

Meet The Mentor

I'm not dying in this phase.

You are not what? *(Big laughter.)* Sorry I can't hear you.

I said "I'm not going to die in this act."

You're not going to die in this act! Are you speaking as The Mentor?

Yes! Yes!

So The Mentor is not going to die in this act. Great! Did you hear that all you Mentors out there?! You're not going to die this act. This is good news! *(Lots of laughter).*

I'm refusing to die. He is not writing me out!

As The Mentor - are you speaking as The Mentor now? Or are you talking as the self?

Well, we're all in agreement.

Okay. I'm going to ask you again to make certain we've all got clarity. May I speak with the voice of The Mentor please, or Controllers, you may step in. Yes?

She didn't want to sign up for this conference, and was reluctant to submit the manuscript, but I forced her to do that.

Okay.

For her own benefit.

So your function is to do what, Mentor?

It's to guide, it's to look after her best interests.

Right. And I also sense that you have to kick her butt from time to time.

Can The Mentor do that then? Doesn't that belong to control?

Am I speaking to The Mentor then?

No, I think I'm being Controller.

All right, okay. That's beautiful. Is it okay if… Would you like to say something as Controller?

I want to know what The Mentor is supposed to do.

Great. You would like to know what The Mentor is supposed to do. Okay, let's ask The Mentor and find out, shall we? So make a little shift in your chair. Okay, that's great. Wonderful. So as The Mentor what do you reckon, not what anybody else says or what Joseph Campbell says, but as The Mentor, as her Mentor, what is your job?

To teach.

To teach. Fantastic.

And I'm willing to make my own sacrifice.

Now did you hear her everybody? She said, "My job is to teach and I'm willing to make my own sacrifice." You, and Gandalf, and Obi-Wan. Very good. Yes?

Well it's kind of the same. To help her. To walk her through the transition, give her the tools to walk through the transition and kick her butt every now and then.

Right. Right. Yes? Remember how testy Gandalf was. Yes?

I provide her with the pictures.

Fantastic. So you provide her with the pictures and make sure she writes the imagery down just right.

I give her the sight and the joy to go further.

Great. So you give her the sight and the joy to go further. To help her go further. There are several voices and I want to get to all of them. Yes?

I have to dare her.

Yeah, great. I think you do! I know this because I coached her a little this morning and I think a bit of challenging will do her good. But you're doing a good job.

I have to give assurance that he can do the work.

You have to give him assurance that he can do the work because the self – when he or she is writing – often loses confidence, don't they?

Yes.

Absolutely. Yes?

I allow her the time and give her permission to be selfish and to take that time.

Great. Very good. Yes?

She doesn't know yet that when I die it's a very good time. It's a wonderful thing when I finally die.

Wow! Did you hear what she said? "She (the self) doesn't know that when I die as The Mentor, it's a very good time." Now can you say a little bit more about that? I think I get it but I'd like to hear you say a little bit more, if that's okay.

When The Mentor – when I die as The Mentor – and she finally doesn't need what I keep trying to show her (and she keeps slamming the door on me) because the realization finally comes in clarity and beauty and awareness of the conflict and finally I can die because she sees it.

Yes! Finally she sees it so you don't have to see it for her anymore. Brilliant. Wonderful. Yes?

I have to give her the opportunity to step forward and try it for herself even though I might think she's too inexperienced to actually do it, but she has to step in there.

Yes, she has to step in there. Absolutely. Because whether the death is literal or metaphorical, she has to do it for herself. Yes, very good.

I need to remind her that she is more than she thinks she is.

You need to remind her, yes! That is one of your primary jobs. "You can do this. You are more than you think you are." That's one of the primary functions of The Mentor, in my view.

I'm going to tell her to be not afraid. And to play to her strengths.

Great.

Despite the fact that...

To be not afraid and to play to her strengths, despite the fact that...

Despite the fact that in her book, despite all the so-called "wisdom" of the Washington authorities, all of their solutions are not working.

Right.

> *It will take at least twenty years before they can solve the economic crisis of this country. She in turn, she lives in Main Street, works in Main Street with these people who are going through this crisis, she knows their pain and more importantly she knows the economics, she understands all of the commerce and so therefore she should stand up, say what she wants to say and maybe, just maybe, she will solve the economic crisis. (Some cheers and applause in the room).*

Great. That's a Mentor with a lot to say. Okay I've got three minutes to finish up. I've been given the signal. Yes?

> *When I die the torch has been passed.*

When you die, as the Mentor, the torch has been passed.

> *I remind her of her skills but also that I can kind of shape shift and instead of me dying, kill the parts of The Controller that aren't necessary in her trying to control other people.*

Right. So you can encourage her to not be so worried about control, really. I know you said 'kill the Controller' but, I am nicer than that actually. Yes?

> *I would tell him not to give up.*

Not to give up. Could you just tell him now, "don't give up."

Don't give up. Keep writing. It's hard, you're gonna fail, you're gonna fall down, just pick yourself up again. (Sounds of agreement in the room.)

Great. That's fantastic.

And if he gets another rejection letter like he did today, keep submitting.

That's right. Keep submitting. Keep submitting.

I have a question.

Who am I speaking to now, you? Or Controller or who?

I'm the dominant one.

All right, you're stepping up now.

What gives each of these voices, or dimensions or personalities, their credibility? Their expertise? Where does that expertise come from? See what I'm saying?

I don't know. You tell me.

The Mentor? What's that? What has he got? What has The Controller got?

Okay. Let me tell you what. Let me ask The Mentor. I'd like to speak with The Mentor, please. (Silence.) All right let me speak with the Controller, please.

No, no. He's out. He's not quite...

Well then, let me speak with YOU, please. Where does that authority come from?

Umm... My answer would be much more metaphysical than this seminar.

Whoa, whoa, whoa! Don't do a dance of the seven veils, come out and say it. Where does this come from? You're among friends, where does it come from?

It's inherent. We're just made this way.

We're just made this way. That sounds very much like a Mentor speaking. I don't know. Sounds very much like that to me. Yes? One last one.

A Final Word - Almost

This is my Mentor speaking. I'm feeling pretty sad because there is this big long journey ahead of you, but it's worth it.

Now, I just want to clarify this, you are speaking as The Mentor?

Yes.

And you're talking to her, the writer?

Yes.

And could you say it again, nice and loud, and I'm going to repeat it because it's worth everybody hearing this.

I'm feeling sad.

You, as The Mentor, are feeling sad.

Yes, I am. I have a lot of sadness and sorrow because I see the journey that she has before her is a long one and a hard one, but it's a journey she has to make.

"I see the journey you have before you," says The Mentor, "I see it. It makes me sad because it's going to be hard, but this is a journey you have to make."

That's right.

Well, writers, I've come to the end of my time today. And I can't think of any better advice to leave you with than the advice you have just given yourself. You know, in Zen terms they would ask the question, "Who writes?" For the last hour or so I've been speaking to whoever that is, the different aspects of you, the Writer. So, as a wise mystic once said, "Be who you are." Keep writing. Thank you.

Epilogue

The Journey into Shadow

The Journey into Shadow

Every story is ultimately the account of a journey into Shadow, a voyage to a 'heart of darkness' where an Enemy holds captive whatever treasure the Hero seeks. This is where the Princess is imprisoned, the gold is buried, the secret formula, amulet or elixir is hidden, guarded by dragons and hedged round with thorns.

Looked at in terms of Plot, The Shadow is the force of external resistance that generates the central conflict of the story. Without The Shadow, there would be no Bad Guy. No Villain, no Antagonist, nothing to threaten and attack the Hero and no real tale to tell. The stronger the Shadow, the more Heroes will be tested, the deeper they will have to dig into themselves and the stronger, cleverer, more courageous and resourceful they will have to be to win through. So, as far as plot is concerned, The Shadow is a device that authors use to put Heroes in jeopardy and make us care about their fate. But there's another side to it.

Psychologist Carl Jung used the term "Shadow" to describe a part of our psychology. And this, it turns out, has implications for our understanding of drama. For Jung, the Shadow was neither villain nor hero, neither Good nor Evil. It was the 'place' in us where we hide the parts of us that make us feel 'bad' about ourselves; the parts that we feel too ashamed, guilty or vulnerable to allow others to see. From this perspective, The Shadow is more than an external Antagonist who opposes the Hero in the Plot; it's also an internal Adversary: a defining part of the Hero's Character. This internal Shadow is an invisible opponent made up of the disowned anger, desire, greed, jealousy, ambition, love, altruism, loyalty – indeed any aspect of the Hero's self that he or she does NOT want to acknowledge – good or bad. In the Shadow lies the inner resource Heroes need, but cannot bring themselves to use, indeed hate themselves for having at all. And this mechanism – the suppression of our unwanted selves and the inner conflict it generates – is crucial to understanding how The Shadow works, not only in fiction, but in life. It is both an obstacle and a resource at the same time.

When Grace Kelly's character in High Noon saves her husband by shooting his enemy in the back, she's no longer the woman she was. The drama has driven her to sacrifice her 'good' Quaker self and reclaim the suppressed, violent side of her nature. When Scrooge wakes up on Christmas morning and saves Tiny Tim, he's no longer a "squeezing, grasping covetous old sinner." The drama has compelled him to abandon greed and mistrust and reclaim his disowned capacity to love.

Thus, change in drama has a very particular meaning: it's the story of how we get bigger by including the rejected parts of ourselves. Yes, the Hero fights the bad guy 'out there' in the world, but, to prevail, he must ultimately reclaim his 'bad', disowned self.

Even in the case of adventure stories, where action and plot trump character and psychology, this way of looking at the Shadow still holds true. Luke Skywalker may have rejected his father's values but he still has to "use the Force," just like his 'evil' father, Darth Vader, did. So in thinking about dramas, real and fictional, we become aware of the qualities we have buried in The Shadow and the choice we will ultimately have to face when our moment of truth comes. Do we have the courage to take responsibility for our Shadow side? Are we willing to be vulnerable and own up to who we really are, warts and all? Are we able to see our Change Journey through to the end – and actually change the way we think and behave?

Earlier, I mentioned that The Four Crises model came out of my research into organizational change and leadership. As I looked at how change worked in that domain, I noticed that the way an organization handled its Shadow side had real implications for its survival – just as it did for the fictional characters we've looked at in this book. I call this phenomenon "Hyde's Law."

If you remember in Robert Louis Stevenson's short story, the hero, Dr. Henry Jekyll, creates a potion to separate his Good from his Evil self. Although he seeks to bring about the dominion of Good, he creates just the opposite. In the end, the dark, misshapen, Evil Mr. Hyde takes over the doctor's personality and kills them both. The same thing applies in organizational life. When an institution identifies only with its "good" public face – and denies the behavior it practices behind the scenes – it will wake up one day to find the most crippling and destructive elements of its management culture have taken control. As Harvard

Professor Chris Argyris has observed, topics will become undiscussible, people will become skillfully unaware of difficult issues and the organization will lurch into a vicious cycle of escalating error, skillful incompetence and desperate fixes that only make matters worse. The fate of energy giant Enron is but one of many examples of this. And Hyde's Law holds as true for us as individuals as it does for corporations and nations. If you don't choose to take ownership of your Shadow, it will take ownership of you and destroy even your most idealistic, high minded projects. Just like Mr. Hyde did with Dr. Jekyll.

This lesson is one of the most humbling aspects of our encounter with The Shadow. It's not just a passive receptacle for our unwanted personality traits. It's an active force, a character in our life story with a mind of its own. It can't really be hidden or buried – at least, not for long. It will not 'go gentle into that good night.' It will just go underground where it will wreak havoc. In times of conflict, we project our Shadow outward and it appears to be our Enemy 'out there' in the world, but it's not. It's us. Or, at least, a vital part of us that we refuse to acknowledge. And the more we delude ourselves into thinking we have nothing to do with it, the more surely and invisibly we allow The Shadow, our inner Mr Hyde, to take control.

So when the plot thickens in your life and you meet difficulty and obstacles on your own creative quest, be it writing a book, building a team, or leading a change for others, give some thought to Walt Kelly's timeless wisdom from the Okefenokee Swamp:

Pogo © Okefenokee Glee and Perloo, Inc. Used by permission

And ponder, with Pogo, what 'shadowy' bit of yourself you may be confronting 'out there' in the world and what that may mean for you.

Afterward

The Four Crises of Leadership

Holding a Mirror up to Nature

Acknowledgements

The Four Crises of Leadership

That this book is addressed primarily to writers is a happy accident. When I began thinking about the ideas explored here, I was about as far away from the problems of writers as I could be. At least I thought I was. It's true, I was thinking about drama, but not in the context of fiction or the people who wrote it. I was thinking about it in terms of leadership. Leadership in real life. I was pouring over a dozen interviews with change leaders, looking at the conflicts they faced and wondering if I could make sense of them as dramas. That is to say, not by using psychology or management science, but *Star Wars*, *Scrooge* and *Oedipus Rex*. Did the principles of dramatic narrative that made stories like these work in fiction, tell us anything about leadership in real life? I discovered, to my surprise, that they did.

I discovered that the very architecture of dramatic stories mirrored the progression of conflicts that leaders face in the real world. I found I could use dramatic structure to map four critical moments of truth, make-or-break crises that leaders would face on their quest to bring about change in real life. Each distinct crisis demanded that leaders use a different set of skills and behaviors, playing different archetypal roles at different times in the change drama. Some leaders seemed to know, as if by instinct, how to do this. Most, did not. Perhaps this was why organizational change so often failed. I realized that by using the Change Journey Process, I could provide leaders with insight into their journey and help them prepare for the kinds of challenges they, and their organizations, would face.

In an upcoming book based on those original interviews with change leaders, I present this model in depth. I look at the structure of drama and illustrate how it works in fiction and then in real life. I give examples from the corporate world and my own experience as a leader. I share practical tools to help leaders navigate each of the crises. In the next few pages, for those who may want to know how the principles of story structure I've been discussing can help leaders better prepare for the challenges they face, I present this brief outline.

The Crisis of Disruption

Calls and Refusals

The first crisis a leader will face involves disrupting the status quo. In myth, as we've seen, this role is played by the archetypal Herald.

The Herald's function in a story is to challenge and warn. To shake things up. Heralds break into the routines of ordinary life to set stories in motion. Leaders perform this function when they call people to the adventure of change. As Heralds, leaders disrupt the group's routines and expose its dysfunctions. They challenge cultural assumptions and the powers that be. They warn of impending threats and point out opportunities. As a rule, they are resisted. Often they are attacked. Successful leaders must persevere for months, sometimes years, to get their point across. Sometimes it takes a crisis like the threat of closure, job loss, or even bankruptcy, to convince people to take change seriously. Whatever the catalyst, if leaders persevere and overcome refusal and resistance, they awaken recognition of the need to change. And with this realization, they ignite another crises: people's fear. If things change... "What will happen to my job? My budget? My Power? What am I going to lose?"

The Crisis of Direction:

Dealing with Fear

"Fear is the mind-killer," wrote Frank Herbert in *Dune*. It's hard to argue with that. Once fear gets a grip on an organization, it will not only kill reason, but friendship, flexibility and trust. It will also provoke a dazzling display of avoidance behaviors and sabotage. So the second crisis involves dealing with fear.

Often leaders see the path ahead so clearly that they find it hard to understand why other people can't do the same. It's tempting to see those who resist change as the 'enemy' without seeing the fear that drives their behavior. This is a serious mistake. Calls to Adventure generate refusal. Storytellers have known this since the beginning of time. In real life, successful leaders learn to respect refusal, even when the case for change seems clear as day. To win cooperation and resolve this crisis, leaders step out of the role of Herald and adopt a different set of behaviors: those of the archetypal Mentor.

In mythic stories, Mentors enter the action to help protagonists deal with their fear. Mentors advise and guide. They identify what needs to be done and why. They clarify the risks and rewards of the journey and prepare protagonists for the road ahead. "First, you've got to take the fear out," one executive told me, "because all of it is fear, fear of the Unknown." Another said, "You don't change people's attitudes and behavior by cold logic or analysis. You've got to understand what makes them move and tick and what's in it for them." So, as Mentors, leaders listen as much as they talk. This does not mean they suffer fools gladly. When they speak, they speak directly and expect directness in return. They develop a vision that makes sense to those who must undertake the journey. They develop practical plans to make it happen and reward systems to reinforce it. Most importantly, they connect people to universal human values and awaken their belief in themselves. In short, they treat their people like the Heroes they must become if change is to work. Leaders who accomplish this enable their organizations to move forward to the next stage of the story. Those who do not, leave their organizations demoralized and mired in chaos – often worse off than when they began.

The Crisis of Commitment:

Leading by Example

The next crisis the leader will face involves gaining commitment to action. Visions, speeches and plans are never enough. People need to see those in authority take action, just as they are being asked to do. When leaders fail this test, people will not commit themselves. They'll duck and dive and avoid the challenge just as their leaders are doing. No amount of rationalizing, blame or fancy foot work will change this.

In the Crisis of Commitment, leaders are called to master their own fear and step into The Hero's role. It's a difficult, sometimes dangerous choice. Confronting powerful adversaries, enforcing threats, challenging phony commitment, surfacing conflict, telling the truth about an issue, drawing the line with a workforce, honoring difficult promises, accepting criticism and feedback – whatever it is, leaders inspire positive action by example, by their willingness to enter into the drama and subject themselves to the same risks as everyone else. Leaders who cannot take this step will never gain commitment to change. But take note.

Effective leaders take up the Hero's role for one reason only: to gain the commitment of their people and to inspire them to become Heroes themselves. Leaders who cannot give up the Hero role, demoralize their organizations. As a leader, it's often hard to realize that the change story does not belong to you. It belongs to the people you lead. Your job is to gain their commitment to a new future. Theirs, to bring that new future into being.

The Crisis of Transformation:

Making the Sacrifice

In the final crisis of change, often after years of work and within sight of success, the forces of antagonism will erupt with unexpected intensity. Here, both leader and organization will face their final test, their ultimate moment of truth.

It might be an unforeseen financial revelation, a disruptive change in the market, a merger or hostile takeover, interference from head office, resignation of a key ally, or just plain exhaustion – whatever it is, this crisis will challenge everyone involved. In the end, both leaders and followers will find they must make a seemingly impossible choice and become the kinds of people they never thought they could be. In one case from my research, a factory general manager shook up both head office and unions to resolve this crisis. He opened up the books – to everyone. All the stakeholders could now see who was paid what, the costs of change so far, the progress they'd made and the final challenge they faced. It galvanized their efforts. In the end, a factory that had begun its change journey facing closure, transformed its working practices, retained 97% of its original workforce, and became one of its company's most prized assets.

The Crisis of Transformation is the final step that releases the organization's true capacity to change. If both leader and the people in the organization pass this test, the new future becomes sustainable and the organization has a good shot at continued adaptation and survival. If not, it will almost certainly fail.

Holding a Mirror Up to Nature

When I took chemistry in high school, I learned that "an atom is like a 'miniature solar system' with electrons whizzing around a nucleus like tiny planets around the sun." It turns out this is a lie. Atoms are not like that at all. The truth is that atoms are not exactly *like* anything, really. According to quantum physics, they're a collection of "probability functions." Now as accurate a description as this may be, "probability functions" would not have gotten me a B in chemistry – which was a miracle given my low aptitude for the subject. No. What got me a B in chemistry was the 'solar system' thing. OK, it wasn't accurate. It wasn't even true, really. But, it was useful. It helped me solve problems. It was, as I'd learned in freshman English, a metaphor, a figure of speech, a linguistic model that helps you understand something you don't know by vivid comparison to something you do know.

Metaphors are more than 'literary devices.' They're conceptual lenses that bring some ideas into sharp focus and blur others, mirrors that have the virtue of limiting what they reflect, so we can get a clearer idea of what we're really looking at. Metaphors may not be true in the way "probability functions" are, but they do capture an aspect of the truth, and that is often more important than any literal description.

An atom is not a solar system any more than the world is 'a stage' or life is 'a brief candle', but metaphors like these are illuminating nonetheless. They give us new ways of seeing the challenges we face. Often, they can help us act more effectively. My goal in this book has not been to reveal any ultimate truth about the creative process or storytelling or leadership, but to hold up the mirror of drama in hopes that what you see reflected in this particular looking-glass will open up new perspectives in your thinking. It certainly has for me.

Acknowledgements

I feel deeply grateful for the inspiration, teaching, feedback, support and encouragement of the following people.

First, I want to thank Hal and Sidra Stone, creators of the Voice Dialogue process. Although I've never met them, their work influenced me profoundly and provided me with some of the basic tools I used to create this book. I first experienced Voice Dialogue in the early 1990's as a client and later a student of Esther Zahniser who trained directly with the Stones. Working with her, I experienced the power of the Voice Dialogue process and the influence of a master facilitator. Whatever skill I may now have in the technique is due to her example, wisdom and insight. For those who would like to know more about Voice Dialogue itself, I recommend the Stone's book *Embracing Ourselves* the original Voice Dialogue training manual or a visit to their website: www.voicedialogueinternational.com

Second, I would like to thank American Zen Master Genpo Merzel Roshi, the creator of the *Big Mind* process. Although he originally developed it to make the experience and understanding of Zen more accessible to the Western Mind, Genpo's innovative approach to Voice Dialogue goes far beyond that. It demonstrates that it's possible to facilitate, not just the subpersonalities of an individual, but also the systemic voices of a group. His work inspired me to develop ways to explore an organization's system of beliefs and behaviors and allow the Shadow aspects of its culture to speak, helping its people surface unspoken conflicts and unravel complex, previously intractable problems. Genpo has expanded the horizons of the Stone's work into areas of spiritual practice, experiential education and beyond and is himself a brilliant facilitator and inspiring teacher. You'll find further information about him and the continuing evolution of *Big Mind* technique on his website: www.bigmind.org

Third, I owe an enormous debt of gratitude to an array of mentors and allies on this quest: to Tony Page, my collaborator in the original 'Four Crises' research; Mats

Hellerstedt-Thorin who first introduced me to Vogler's work; Jamie Moran, my longtime friend and colleague for our countless illuminating discussions about the meaning of Drama; to Jim Misko for inviting me to speak in Alaska and to the Alaska Writer's Guild itself for welcoming me and entering so fully into our dialogue; to Shirley Kressel without whose prompting this book would never have reached the page; to her husband, Herb for his much needed advice and support in a crisis; to Deanna Rallo, my copy editor, for her assiduous pursuit of my wandering punctuation and patchy grammar; to my pre-publication readers, especially Stella Duffy and Shelley Silas for their inspiring confidence in this book and in life; and to my life time mentors past and present: David Hardy, Dan Fauci, Viola Spolin, Mike Alfreds, Dennis Palumbo, and Ingemar and Birgitta Thorin. Their example and inspiration are a constant reminder to me of the healing power of The Creative.

Lastly, I want to thank my beautiful wife and lifelong companion Anita Harmon, therapist, poet, and teacher; my first reader and best critic, for our running 50 year argument about the nature of love.

CHANGE JOURNEY

About the Author

Andy Harmon is a theatre director and playwright who stepped from the stage into management consulting in the late 1980's when Price Waterhouse in London asked him to train their consultants to deliver more memorable change workshops. Along with his wife, psychologist Anita Harmon, he went on to develop programs that use acting skills to help people in organizations negotiate, sell, influence and lead more effectively. His work with Price Waterhouse Coopers, IBM, McKinsey and Co, The Body Shop, British Telecom and many other clients including two UK Government Departments, led him to develop a unique approach to personal development, based on the archetypes of drama and mythic stories, to help leaders at every level surmount the challenges of change. If you've found this book helpful and wish to learn more about how Andy's work can help you or your organization, please email him at andy@actorsmind.com or visit the Actors Mind or Change Journey websites:

www.actorsmind.com   www.changejourney.net

Made in the USA
Las Vegas, NV
07 December 2024